MW00577657

HOW TO GET A
UX DESIGN JOB

Create a compelling portfolio, submit a
stand-out application, and ace the interview
to land your user experience dream job

LISA MURNAN

Cover and Book Design by Jenn Paul Glaser

 **UX FOR THE PEOPLE**

March 2018

How to Get a UX Design Job
by Lisa Murnan

Copyright © *2018* Lisa Murnan. All rights reserved.

Printed in the United States of America.

Published by UX for the People
Pine, Colorado

ISBN: 978-0-9886304-2-0 (paperback)
ISBN 978-0-9886304-4-4 (ebook)

How to Get a UX Design Job may be purchased for educational, business or sales promotional use. Online editions can be ordered through the Amazon website.

Additional resources are available on Lisa Murnan's website *(http://lisamurnan.com/resources).*

Typefaces: Adobe Garamond Pro and Viato

The UX for the People logo © is proprietary to Lisa Murnan.

Cover and Book Design by Jenn Paul Glaser of Scribe Arts for Our Planet, Oceans and Fisheries *(https://www.scribearts.org)*

For my students, who remind me why I love UX.

Table of Contents

Intro

We are in the midst of a "UX Gold Rush," according to *Forbes*.

The signs are everywhere. "UX Designer" is now included on Glassdoor's influential "50 Best Jobs in America" list (ranked 27th in 2018). Searching on the keyword "UX" on any of the major job sites will yield thousands of results. And LinkedIn now has over 110,000 members with "UX" in their job title (compared to 159 members in 2008 and 3,500 in 2013).

This all sounds great if you're looking to transition from your current job into a user experience career, right? The problem is, many companies want UX professionals with at least two to three years of experience. There's a huge demand for UX designers, but it's a demand for mid-level and senior designers. Junior positions are harder to find, and the competition is fierce (partially because of the tidal wave of junior-level designers emerging from UI/UX design certificate programs like General Assembly, Springboard, etc.). What's an aspiring UXer to do?

You need to find a way to fit in (on one hand) and stand out (on the other) so that you can get your foot in the door and start working in the industry. This book will help you do that.

If you're an experienced UXer, it's a whole new world out there. A few years ago, nobody was requesting our portfolios or grilling us with behavioral interview questions or asking us to spend 45 minutes on a whiteboard explaining how we'd design an elevator for a 1,000-floor building. Whether you're actively looking for a new gig or just constantly barraged by recruiters trying to lure you to greener pastures, you need to be prepared. Portfolios (good ones, anyway) aren't created overnight.

This book will tell you what today's recruiters and hiring managers are looking for in good job candidates (at all experience levels), and what you can expect during the recruiting and interview process.

You'll need to create a resume that will pass the Applicant Tracking System (ATS) test and a UX portfolio that is slick enough to impress recruiters during the initial screening process (and substantial enough to get you in front of the hiring manager).

You'll also need a solid online presence, including social media profiles and a website that shows you in the best light.

Then you'll have to really turn on the charm and walk the walk during the interviews, portfolio presentations, and design exercises.

There are no silver bullets. I'm not going to tell you to create a video resume or to print your resume on pink perfumed paper. No tricks here. You're going to have to take action and bust your ass.

You can do it, though. You're going to treat this whole job hunt process like a UX project and I'll show you how.

I know it can feel overwhelming. I've been doing UX work since before it was called UX, and I still feel like an imposter sometimes. I even wonder if, after 23 years in the industry, I'd make it through some of today's screening processes and interviews and design exercises.

I'll let you in on a little secret. Most of us senior UXers are self-taught and had to learn UX the hard way – stressful project after stressful project. We spent years learning from our mistakes and by talking to users, collaborating with other UXers and stake-holders, and watching usability tests. There aren't many better ways to learn than by seeing your design get torn apart during a usability test!

I was introduced to web design in 1994 when I was working at a newspaper in North Carolina. Management gathered up all the tech-savvy people at the newspaper (I was a news researcher and spent a lot of time on LexisNexis), put us in a group called New Media, and sent us off to another building to create an online version of the newspaper. So I learned to code HTML by sitting next to a guy who knew HTML, and I learned to crop photos and create graphics in Photoshop by sitting next to another guy who knew Photoshop.

A year later I landed a job as a webmaster at a software company. I had no idea what I was doing but nobody else knew what I was doing either, so at least I had that going for me. It took me weeks to figure out I could view HTML files in a browser from a local folder on my computer. Seriously. I used to FTP files up to the server just to look at them in a browser.

Back then the Internet was the Wild West. There was no pro-cess. There were no UX classes and hardly any books or mentors. The best sources of knowledge I had were usability guru Jakob Nielsen's articles and reports (which I still read today), and decon-structing other people's websites.

Today there are so many different ways you can learn about UX. Immersive in-person courses, online classes, books, blogs, YouTube videos, Meetups, conferences, and millions of websites for inspiration. There are lots of great tools, too – Axure, Sketch, InVision, Balsamiq, design templates and libraries out the wazoo, online card sorting apps, WordPress and all its plugins, Google Analytics, and Slack.

Maybe this is why some of us old-timers act a little curmudgeonly toward younger designers sometimes.

A year ago I started teaching the UI/UX design certificate program at Boulder Digital Arts. The class is held several times a year in person in Boulder, CO. I love teaching this class. I think I learn as much from my students as they learn from me.

My students are from all walks of life – they are graphic designers, developers, illustrators, photographers, writers, marketing people, product managers, salespeople, college students. Their ages range from the early 20s to late 50s. One thing they all have in common is that they are strongly drawn to UX. Many of them are already experimenting with UX design in their current jobs. They're putting in a significant amount of free time to explore UX concepts and work on design projects. They are trying to figure out if they want to pursue a full-time UX career.

There is so much to try to pack into a 40-hour class, and we spend a lot of time designing and collaborating on student projects, so all the finer details of UX portfolios, resumes, interviewing, etc. often get pushed out to the very end, and by then everybody is brain-dead.

I wrote this book to bridge that gap. I started out by giving my students access to a Google drive full of cheat sheets, but a book seemed so much more *useful*. Plus a book allows me to share this knowledge with a much bigger audience than the ~30 students I teach every year. It has become a personal mission of mine to help as many people who truly love UX find a user experience design job that makes them happy.

So is it all worth it, trying to get a job in UX? *Yes*. You get to solve problems and make people's lives better. There's a great sense of satisfaction in fixing things or making complicated things easier to use. You get to work with a lot of cool people. Often you can wear what you want (creative people can get away with a lot), work from home, and the pay is good. It's fun being a UX designer. You get to have an "X" in your title and be all edgy and shit. *Yo*.

Disclaimer! The purpose of this book is not to teach you how to be a good UX designer. If you're looking for UX jobs I assume you've already got this part covered. There are tons of great books out there that cover UX concepts, process, strategy, skills, tools, etc. This book is about helping you get a job.

Ok, ready to get to work? Let's do this.

[1]

What Hiring Managers Are Looking For

Background

Your background doesn't seem to matter that much. For the longest time, there was no such thing as a UX degree (now there are schools like Jared Spool's Center Centre and more established colleges offering interaction design and UX design degrees), so we all started out from different backgrounds. You'll see UXers with degrees in liberal arts, psychology, philosophy, English (my degree), computer science, design, business, etc.

Wait, Do I Need a College Degree?

We're seeing the need for it less and less. As I was researching this section I came across a "Lead UI/UX Designer" posting on Indeed that said: "The only credentials we care about is that you are an expert in doing the things listed above. Graduating summa cum laude from the Rhode Island School of Art is a fantastic data point, but what's more important in our eyes is how well you work with our team, and the caliber of work you consistently deliver. Results speak much louder than words."

Many UX job postings don't mention educational requirements at all, or simply say, "Bachelor's degree or equivalent experience."

According to Glassdoor (in their article "15 More Companies That No Longer Require a Degree – Apply Now"), the following companies do not require a college diploma for some of their "top jobs": Google, Ernst and Young, Penguin Random House, Costco Wholesale, Whole Foods, Hilton, Publix, Apple, Starbucks, Nordstrom, Home Depot, IBM, and Bank of America.

So What *Do* They Want?

It depends.

Some hiring managers will say that having several years of experience under your belt doesn't necessarily mean that you're a good designer. They want to see proof that you are via a portfolio. To them, if you don't have a portfolio it's a non-starter.

Others think there is no substitute for experience, especially when it comes to dealing comfortably with product managers, clients, users, stakeholders, etc., and also when it comes to applying what you've learned from lots of contextual interviews and usability tests. They'll say you can wow somebody with a sexy portfolio but that doesn't prove that you know what you're doing, it just means you're good at designing portfolios.

Then you've got someone like Laszlo Bock (former SVP of People Operations at Google) telling the *New York Times* that the least important attribute Google looks for is "expertise." Instead, they focus on learning ability, leadership, humility, and a sense of ownership.

It seems reasonable to assume that senior-level UX designers will be judged more on their experience and portfolios, while junior-level designers will be judged more on their potential and work ethic.

It really depends on which company you're interviewing with and what they value in a candidate.

Why Hire a Junior Designer?

I was recently asked by one of my students, "Why would a company hire me instead of someone like you (with your years of experience)?"

There are several reasons I can think of.

1. I require a lot more money than a junior UXer.
2. Some UXers get complacent or burned out and quit growing after a while. They don't keep up with the newest tools, they may not understand how responsive design or mobile apps work because the project they've been on hasn't required that of them, they don't network anymore. Their portfolio is dated or nonexistent. Meanwhile, the aspiring UXers are pushing themselves every day to learn and grow and understand the latest design trends. And their enthusiasm and passion for UX comes through in interviews. (Just don't let it come across too much, because that's annoying.)
3. Hiring junior UXers is a good way to leverage the more experienced senior people. Senior designers can delegate some of their tactical work to juniors so they can focus on the bigger more strategic stuff.

In my experience, the types of places that hire junior UXers are:

- **Startups**, who will be looking for a UX generalist (or a "unicorn" who can do *everything* – they may have you answer the phones and write their blog while you are also designing and coding their mobile app).
- **Big corporate UX teams**, especially those who require their employees to work on-site versus remote. They have a limited pool of local talent to choose from and are often willing to take on junior designers because they have a lot of managers

and senior designers there to mentor them. When I was at Ally Financial in 2014, they were hiring print designers with no web experience to join the UX team as visual designers. They had to do this because they needed visual designers ASAP, their UX staff was required to come into the office every day, and the Charlotte market was extremely competitive with big companies like Bank of America, Wells Fargo, Home Depot, TIAA, and others all competing for the same people.

• **Consultancies and agencies**, who often need to put warm bodies in seats to work on incoming projects. This isn't necessarily a bad place for junior UXers to land, though. There are usually lots of mentors around and a variety of fast-paced projects to work on, so you can learn a lot in a short period of time.

If you're a graduate of a UX certificate program, you'll need to find ways to differentiate yourself from the other graduates, because they are all saturating the market right now.

The certificate program I teach requires students to come up with their own project idea and collaborate on it with the class (UX team style), so what each student puts in their portfolio is uniquely their own. Many of the other programs have students all working on the same project. If you're doing a group project that every student in every class has worked on, it's going to come up as a red flag in your portfolio – recruiters or hiring managers have probably seen that project before. It's important that you come up with some work of your very own for your portfolio. We will talk more about this in an upcoming chapter.

From Their Point of View

Although it seems like they're calling all the shots, hiring managers and other potential team members are anxious during the interview process, too. They don't want to make the wrong

recommendation or choice. A poor fit causes all sorts of angst –
the poor fit isn't happy, their coworkers aren't happy, their project
may be suffering, the company has already put all sorts of time
and money into onboarding them and now the hiring manager
has to publicly take responsibility for their bad decision and deal
with the situation. Then they have to find somebody else, fast.

Other UXers may get caught up in comparing themselves to you
when they evaluate you. Do you solve problems the way they
do? Do you use the same tools they do? Do you communicate
the way they do? Do your deliverables look like theirs? This isn't
fair, especially if they're a senior designer and they're interviewing you for a junior position. Ironically, they may hold you to
a higher standard than they were held to when they were hired
– they might not even pass their own interview process if they
were going through it today! (If this happens to you, your best
bet is to demonstrate your knowledge of the UX design process.
Dropping Jakob Nielsen's name might help, too.)

What Do *You* Want?

So now that we (sort of) know what hiring managers are looking
for, what are *you* looking for?

Do you want to be a generalist (aka a "Swiss Army knife" designer,
sometimes confused with a unicorn), who can do lots of different
things like user research, information architecture, interaction
design, and some usability testing (sometimes with a little visual
design or front-end coding thrown in)? Or do you want to be a
specialist who focuses on one skill and really masters it, like user
research or visual design or interaction design?

Do you want to work on a big team, where there are lots of other
designers to collaborate with and learn from, or would you prefer
to work on a small team or even be a UX team of one at a startup

15

or small company? Do you want to work from home or at an office (or both)?

What kinds of projects do you want to work on – web apps, customer portals, branding sites, analytics dashboards, SaaS, retail, mobile apps, media, gaming, security, eLearning, blockchain…? Is there a particular industry you want to be in, like financial services or healthcare or cryptocurrency?

Do you want to do something socially impactful, or are you okay working for "the man" and selling something? A lot of UXers are so good-hearted and truly do like helping people, and I am not being sarcastic when I say that if you get to know your users and empathize with them, you'll soon recognize that you're helping make their jobs easier or their lives better, regardless of what you're building.

I was on a project once where I designed an iPad app that helped Finance & Insurance (F&I) Managers at car dealerships (you know, the guys that sit across from you and push paper after paper for you to sign when you're buying a car) sell customers vehicle service contracts. I got to know several F&I Managers over the course of the project and they were cool and they liked the app we designed. Overall it was an interesting project to work on and the app tested well, which is always rewarding for a designer. I just tried not to think too much about the fact that we were selling vehicle service contracts. (When I was doing early user research for the project and googled "vehicle service contracts," half the results were about what a scam or waste of money they were. Consumer Reports gave them the big thumbs down.)

What do you hate about your current job and hope you never have to do again? What do you like about it? What would you like to be doing in the future?

Make sure that whatever job you take fits into this plan. Don't just take a job because you're running *away* from your current situation, run *toward* something instead.

[2]

Your Job Hunt is a UX Project

Think about the whole job hunt process from a UX point of view. Your job hunt is a project, and you already have everything you need in your toolbox to make this project successful.

On this project, you're the business, and your business goal is to get a UX job. Your resume, portfolio, cover letter, website, social media presence, and in-person interactions (interviews, design exercises, emails, conversations) are all products you're creating to make this goal a reality.

The users are all of the people who will be interacting with these products you create and evaluating you. They have their own goals – they need to fill a job opening and find someone who meets their criteria, will make their lives easier, make their products better, work well with their team, etc. These are recruiters, HR people, hiring managers, potential UX teammates, and other stakeholders.

The user-centered design process that UX designers follow is iterative and involves users throughout the design and development of a product. The names of the phases can vary, but they're generally laid out like this:

Here's what to think about in each phase. We'll get into a lot of the how-to details later in the book.

Discover

This is the phase where you nail down the business objectives and do user research.

- Decide what kind of UX job you actually want.
- Get to know your users (starting with the personas below).
- Deconstruct job postings.
- Look at your "competitors" (other designers' portfolios, LinkedIn profiles, etc.).
- Research the companies you're interested in.
- Google yourself.

Let's look at your users a little more in depth.

RECRUITER – "KATE"

"Being able to play matchmaker and connect a great company with top talent is what truly motivates me as a recruiter!"

Overview	May be in-house (as part of company's HR department) or part of an external recruiting firm Annually reviews thousands of portfolios and interviews hundreds of candidates to find the right match for her clients Works for the employer, not you
Goal	To match talented professionals with opportunities from employers
Pain Points	Race against time – many recruiters searching at the same time for the right candidate Logistical nightmares – phone tag and interview scheduling Not hearing back from candidates Candidates reacting poorly to interview feedback Candidates turning down offers
UX Knowledge	Low

RECRUITER – "KATE"	
Interaction with You	Shepherds you through the interview/hiring process Acts as the primary liaison between you and the company Often your ally, advising you on how to make the best impression Handles administrative details (such as salary, benefits, travel arrangements)

HIRING MANAGER – "ANDREW"	
"It's pretty straightforward - do they have the skills, and do they have the right personality and cultural fit?"	
Overview	Reviews anywhere between 12–50 portfolios for a position Sometimes reviews portfolios on his phone Often removed from day-to-day design decisions Wants you to succeed – if you're the perfect fit, he can hire you and get back to his "real" work
Goal	To hire a UX designer that has the necessary skills to do the job and is a great culture fit
Pain Points	Uncertainty over what parts of the portfolio were actually created by you Long rambling cover letters or badly formatted resumes or portfolios Afraid of making a hiring mistake
UX Knowledge	Medium to high (depends on their background… may be more strategic than tactical)

HIRING MANAGER – "ANDREW"

Interaction with You	Interviews you and introduces you to the rest of the team Makes the final hiring decision Wants to see and hear details about your design experience (usually through a portfolio review) Wants to see how you interact with the team and how you react to design feedback

SENIOR UX DESIGNER (POTENTIAL UX TEAM MEMBER) "MELANIE"

"I wouldn't want to hire a UX designer without seeing them do design work."

Overview	Usually not involved in high-level screening of candidates May or may not have final say over whether somebody is hired, but definitely has influence Would prefer to hire someone she's already worked with or knows personally
Goals	To hire a UX designer who will fit well with the rest of the team To add somebody to the team who can contribute something valuable, either through knowledge/skills or collaboration
Pain Points	Fear that the person they hire won't know what they're doing Afraid of recommending the wrong person
UX Knowledge	High

SENIOR UX DESIGNER (POTENTIAL UX TEAM MEMBER) "MELANIE"	
Interaction with You	Interviews you and provides feedback to recruiter and hiring manager May participate in collaborative design exercise with you Wants to hear about your process in great detail Wants to see examples of your deliverables (like wireframes/prototypes)

SENIOR ENGINEER (POTENTIAL TEAM MEMBER) – "ERIC"

"If you're an engineer without a background in design, hiring a designer can be challenging, frustrating, or downright scary."

Overview	Usually not involved in high-level screening of candidates Probably works with UX peripherally
Goal	To work with a UX designer who understands technical constraints and the importance of efficiency and quality (the less bugs and changes, the better)
Pain Points	Prima donna UX designers who over-design things Not reusing UI patterns so he constantly has to reinvent the wheel
UX Knowledge	Low
Interaction with You	Interviews you and provides feedback to recruiter and hiring manager Wants to hear that you're willing to tweak your design (without compromising the user experience) to help meet deadlines or reduce development work

Define

This is where you'll get things organized.

- Gather your content (for your portfolio, resume, website, LinkedIn profile, etc.). This could include existing resumes or portfolios (yours and other designers'), screenshots and images for your portfolio, links to social media profiles, possibly a logo for your website, a professional-looking headshot, and unique background image for LinkedIn, etc.
- Write down your answers to the most common interview

questions and practice answering them out loud.
- Set up a spot in your house for online interviews and have someone test it with you (using Skype, Google Hangouts, etc.).

Design & Deploy

For the sake of this job hunt project we'll combine the Design and Deploy phases, because you're not going to be doing much sketching/prototyping beforehand, you're just going to be cranking things out (and constantly iterating on them).

This will sound obvious, but as a UX designer you're going to be held to a higher standard than most people when it comes to things like your resume, portfolio, cover letter, and website. They should be attractive and easily scannable. They should contain all of the important information a user would want. They should be typo-free. The fonts and colors should be consistent (on the print versions of your resume and portfolio, for example). They should look every bit as good, or better, than something you'd create for a client.

Don't worry if your visual design skills aren't all that great. Just make everything look clean and professional. Use white space and category groupings and good fonts (no Comic Sans!) and color accents to create compelling "products."

What's included in these phases (again, we'll cover the details on all of these in upcoming chapters):
- Create a resume that is Applicant Tracking System (ATS) friendly.
- Create a pretty resume (PDF format) to email to people that ask for it, and to print out and bring to interviews.
- Create an online portfolio.
- Create a PDF version of your portfolio.

- Complete your LinkedIn profile and turn the recruiter beacon on.
- Go through all your public social media accounts (Twitter, Instagram, Pinterest, etc.) and make sure they look professional and are consistent with each other. If your Facebook account has posts that are visible to the public, make sure there's nothing inappropriate on there.
- Create a personal website (optional).
- Create new content or social media profiles (if necessary) to improve Google search results on your name.
- Test *everything* – read your resume and portfolio out loud to yourself and have friends read through everything for you. You could also join a few UX Meetup groups and share your resume/portfolio with other members.
- Start applying for jobs.

Measure
- Imagine that every interaction (email, interview, etc.) with one of your "users" is user research or a usability test.
- Use Google Analytics to track visits to your website and online portfolio.
- Use LinkedIn's "Profile Views" feature to see who's looking at your profile.
- Check Google to see what comes up when you type in your name (if you've been making changes/additions to your online presence).
- Document all the jobs you apply for – it can be a simple spreadsheet with company name, date applied, and a notes area.
- Document any interview questions you were asked and how you answered them. If there's room for improvement, tweak the wording in your cheat sheet of written questions and answers and practice saying the new answers out loud.

[3]

Where to Look for Jobs

Here are some good places to look for UX jobs.

Indeed

This is my personal favorite because it's so simple and comprehensive. It's a lot like Google, you just type in a keyword or two (with or without a location) and boom, you get all these great results back. Indeed indexes company websites, newspapers, job boards, staffing agencies, etc., so it feels like they've found just about everything.

You can set up easy email alerts that let you know when something new has been added that matches your keywords.

Indeed has an "Upload Your Resume" option that makes it easy to quickly apply for jobs, but don't be tempted. Your resume should be customized for every job you apply for. You don't want to upload a one-size-fits-all resume. More on this in an upcoming chapter.

LinkedIn

LinkedIn is another great place to find jobs, and they have some cool personalization features, such as letting you know if someone in your network already works at a company you're interested in. Since LinkedIn already has all the info you entered into your profile section, they know what jobs you're qualified for based on your skill set and where you live, so they proactively show you jobs you might be interested in.

Another nice feature is that you can look at all the people on LinkedIn who currently work at the company. I usually go into stealth mode (Me > Settings & Privacy > Privacy > Profile viewing options) when I'm researching people at other companies specifically for job hunting. It just feels like I'm stalking them, and I also don't want them checking out my profile (which leads to my website and online portfolio) too early in the process.

If someone in your network works at a company with a job opening you're interested in, it doesn't hurt to ask them if they'll tell you more about the job/company, introduce you to the hiring manager, or even refer you for a particular job. They may be open to it if you look like a strong candidate, because many companies offer a nice fat referral fee to employees whose referrals get hired. At my current company, referral fees can range from $2,500 to $5,000 depending on the role.

LinkedIn has a new feature where you can turn on a little beacon letting recruiters know that you're open to discussing new opportunities. If you go to your own profile, there will be a dashboard at the top (under your photo and summary). There you can toggle on the recruiter beacon (LinkedIn says that they will block recruiters from your current company from seeing it. I'm not sure how fail-safe that is, but I think the gains outweigh the risks.) There is also a link there to see who's been viewing your profile recently.

You can easily apply for jobs through LinkedIn, and they'll pull information straight from your profile and send it to employers, but again – don't be tempted! Create a customized resume instead and apply directly with the employer.

All of the things I just mentioned are available for free – you don't need to be a member of their Premium service to take advantage of them. Take the time to fill out every section of your profile and customize it wherever you can (add a headshot, add a unique background image, etc.). It really does help. It also helps to post a status update or to "like," comment on, or share posts that you find interesting on your newsfeed. Doing this keeps your name in front of people. Don't go too crazy with it, though, because people in your network get notifications about even the stuff you just "liked." Be selective.

Meetups

We have a lot of UX Meetup groups around me (in the Denver/ Boulder area). They meet regularly and have all sorts of great topics for their meetings, plus frequent guest speakers.

Several of the groups also use Slack to stay in touch in between meetings, and all of their Slack workspaces have a #jobs channel. It's a great way to find out about local jobs that have just been posted, and the people who post them (usually other UX employees at the company) are happy to answer questions about the job.

Glassdoor

Although Glassdoor usually has the same job postings as Indeed and LinkedIn, they include a salary estimate on the job posting that the others don't, based on real salaries (for that company/ role/industry) submitted by the Glassdoor community.

In addition to salary information, Glassdoor also has anonymous reviews submitted by company employees and interview questions that candidates were actually asked during interviews at the company. This information can be unbelievably helpful.

I saw a job posting for a User Experience Design Manager a few months ago that looked amazing – my skills were a perfect match for almost every bullet point of the job description and it would have been a promotion for me.

And then…I read the Glassdoor reviews. I sorted them by date so that I'd be reading the most recent ones first, and they were devastating. I finally stopped when I read this line: "The sheer incompetence and all-out political culture of the VP level and down is downright comical at times if it weren't for the fact that it chews up passionate employees and spits out zombies." Wow. No wonder they had job openings.

We Work Remotely

We Work Remotely (weworkremotely.com) is owned by Tiny, the same company that owns Dribbble. The website, which is currently a simple one-page listing of jobs, promotes a variety of remote opportunities, including UI/UX-related jobs in the "Design" section. I have a feeling this site is going to explode over the next couple of years.

A Note About Networking

Some people will insist that networking is the be-all end-all only-all way to get a good UX job, but I'm here to tell you it's not true.

I landed two of my last three full-time UX jobs by submitting an application on each company's website and going through the entire process pretty much as I describe it in this book. I was not recruited for either job and I didn't know anybody at either company beforehand.

That's not to say that you shouldn't network! By all means, network. It will definitely increase your chances. But don't feel like you have to follow every prominent UX person on Twitter and attend every Meetup in your area.

One easy and painless way to network is to compliment people on things they created that you enjoyed, like their book, blog post, article, video, online class, in-person presentation, etc.

You can send a brief private message or do something more public, like tag them on Twitter or LinkedIn while mentioning their creation. If you have an intelligent question to ask them about what you read/watched, even better.

Reaching out to people this way is far less intimidating than talking to them at an event (at least it is for me, the introverted recluse who lives in the mountains). Plus, they're more likely to remember you.

Also, don't neglect your existing network. Don't be that asshole that nobody hears from until they need something. It doesn't take much to stay in touch and it doesn't have to be forced or insincere. Engage with people's posts on social media. Wish them a happy birthday. Congratulate them on promotions or accomplishments. Be a friend.

Don't Sell Yourself Short

If you don't meet all of the criteria in a job posting, apply anyway! Most teams have a Must Have list and a Nice to Have list, and it will often be very difficult for them to find somebody that matches every single bullet point (and if they do, they might not be able to afford them).

Some companies get too picky with requirements, asking for very specific design tools or industry-specific knowledge, and then they end up with a narrow group of candidates to select from and have to widen their search. If you match ~80% of the criteria, I say go for it.

[4]

Deconstructing Job Postings

When creating any of the "products" discussed in this book – your resume, portfolio, cover letter, etc. – familiarize yourself with each job posting and parse out specifically what they are asking for, so you can customize accordingly. Most of the job descriptions ask for the same high-level set of UX skills, deliverables, and tools knowledge, but then also include some unique requirements for their particular role or product or industry.

First, a Note About Unicorns

If you google "UX unicorn" you will find some funny definitions, including this one from uxunicorn.com:

> *"Mythical user experience designer with an advanced and adaptive skill range. Outstanding skills in graphic design, rapid prototyping, front end development, user testing, technical specifications, marketing and branding. It does not have an opinion, it has a process, and will harmonize with any environment."*

UX designers are already expected to do so much, from helping to define business requirements to participating in user research, coming up with the site structure and flow, creating wireframes and/or prototypes, participating in the testing of those prototypes, and presenting design ideas to executives and stakeholders. I believe visual design and coding fall outside the UX designer's purview. Visual design and front-end development each require a very specialized set of skills and are easily full-time jobs all on their own.

If you happen to have visual design or coding skills, that's great. It'll add to your mystique. I just don't think it's fair for companies to expect it as part of a UX designer position.

Here's an example from Indeed:

> *"Our Product Development team is working on the next big startups and tech innovations, and we're in search for a UX unicorn. <Company name> is looking for a UX Designer who can contribute to all aspects of product strategy and design, including ideation, research, interaction design and visual design. If this is you, keep reading!"*

When I read a job description like this, I feel the weight of the world on my shoulders (at least this company doesn't also expect you to code all your own prototypes into production-quality HTML, CSS, and JavaScript). This looks like a position where you'll be doing everything and getting very little support or collaboration opportunities with other UXers.

Titles
UX titles are all over the place. It's like watching a roulette wheel, and right now the little white ball seems to be settling on "UX Designer." I've been an information architect (IA), interaction designer (IxD), and UX designer (UXD), and all of those roles have been very similar to each other.

Although "UX Designer" and "Interaction Designer" are often used interchangeably in job postings, interaction design is technically more focused on the UI (how the screens work together and how users interact with them) while UX design is broader and more strategic. UX is the umbrella term and interaction design falls underneath it.

An "Information Architect" organizes information and creates navigational structures. This role is evolving into something more specialized and technical, and it's rare to see it confused with UX designer anymore.

In fact, a recruiter recently contacted me about an information architect position and here's what part of the description said: "A lot of this will be figuring out how information should flow. Looking for someone with a design background so they understand what is possible conceptually, but they will not be doing the actual design."

Some companies are confused about the various UX roles (and who can blame them) so they'll ask for something different from what they mean. For example, my current position was listed as a "Usability Engineer." I would never consider myself to be a usability engineer, but when I read through the job description it was exactly what I was already doing as an information architect/interaction designer. I think they called it "Usability Engineer" because it had the word "engineer" in it and the role was going to live inside the engineering organization.

When you're searching for jobs, branch out a bit and search on other keywords like "wireframes" or even specific tool names like InVision, because you may find a job title/description without "UX" in it. And hey, you might be the only person who's able to find it, so you'll have a much better chance of getting through the screening process.

Some of the UX-related titles I saw on Indeed:
- UX Designer
- Lead UI/UX Designer Rockstar (I am not making this up)
- UX/IxD Designer
- User Experience/UX Designer
- UX Designer/Researcher
- UX Architect
- UX Researcher
- Usability Engineer
- Experience Designer
- Product Designer
- Interaction Designer
- Information Architect
- Digital UX Architect

All of them had very similar job descriptions, although the "UX Researcher" and "Usability Engineer" postings emphasized user research and usability testing activities more heavily than prototyping and design.

Common Requirements

For this chapter, I reviewed approximately 30 UX job postings on Indeed (I put "UX" into the keyword field and left the location blank). Anything below with quotes around it was pulled directly from one of those job postings.

> *"Bring strong creative, conceptual and problem-solving skills to translate conceptual ideas, business needs and user goals into interaction and design solutions"*

That requirement pretty much sums up what UXers do on a day to day basis. As UXers, it's our job to:
1. Work with companies/clients to understand what their goals

are and what our constraints (time, budget, platform, etc.) are.
2. Understand who the end-users of the product are (through a variety of user research methods) and what their goals and pain points are.
3. Come up with design solutions that make both the business and users happy (which you'll know because you did usability testing).

At its heart, UX is about creative problem solving. It's about making things as easy to use as possible. It's about helping everybody achieve their goals.

> *"Collaborate closely with product management, engineering, software development, visual design, branding, and business operations to establish practices for designing end-to-end experiences that are meaningful to our users and valuable to the business."*

Collaborating with and communicating our ideas to other designers and stakeholders is a critical UX skill. The best designs are created through extensive research, collaboration, iteration, and testing, not by being some "genius designer" off on your own somewhere designing in a bubble.

> *"Create and effectively present UX artifacts....*
> *to explain and negotiate design solutions to key stakeholders."*

The wording will vary and some companies will ask for obscure things (I saw one post asking for "mind maps" which I have never created in 23 years of UXing), but the most common UX deliverables are:

- **Wireframes and Prototypes.** I use these terms interchangeably out of years of habit, but in general I consider a *wireframe* to be a flat representation of a screen (often with placeholder text and images) and a *prototype* to be an interactive series of screens (or dynamic actions on one screen). Both are generally created in a prototyping software like Axure, Sketch, or Balsamiq. These are by far the most sought-after UX deliverables.
- **Personas.** Realistic character sketches that represent audience segments or customer types. Usually contain a stock photo and various sections that describe that persona (goals, pain points, etc.). Can be done in a variety of programs – Word, PowerPoint, InDesign, Photoshop, etc.
- **User Scenarios.** A "day in the life" of a persona. Often included as part of the original persona document (sometimes as page two of a persona).
- **User/Task Flows.** Define how the user navigates through a website or app to complete a goal, and/or how a user completes a specific task step-by-step. Often done on a whiteboard or with Post-it Notes on a wall. Can also be represented by flowchart diagrams.
- **Site Maps.** Show the hierarchical organization of a website or app's content. They often look like org charts or family trees. Each box on a sitemap is meant to represent a page (or a type of page, like a news article).
- **Customer Journey Maps.** High-level views of the end-to-end experience a customer has with a product, including all the different touchpoints they have with the company.
- **Storyboards.** A way to visually describe a user's experience using illustrations inside frames, arranged like a comic book.
- **User research output.** This can be from contextual interviews, competitive/comparative analysis, surveys, focus groups, card sorts, heuristic reviews, etc.
- **Usability test output.** Quantitative (data/metrics) and

qualitative (observational) results from usability testing.

- **Visual design comps.** Pixel-perfect final designs, usually created in Adobe Photoshop or Illustrator and handed off to developers in the Deploy stage. Usually produced by a visual designer, not a UX designer.

> *"A strong portfolio...demonstrating experience and relevant, user-centered designs"*

Hiring managers want to see your portfolio. Some companies won't even consider you unless you have one. Per Google:

> *"Please include URLs for an online portfolio in addition to resume. Submissions without a portfolio included will not be considered."*

Skills, Responsibilities, Requirements, Competencies, etc.

FLUFF TALK

A lot of postings are padded with Captain Obvious statements, marketing-speak, and industry buzzwords. Not to say that soft skills (like communication, writing, being a good team player, attention to detail, etc.) aren't important, just that most of them are no-brainers and would be hard to work into a resume or portfolio without sounding weird.

Here are some examples:
- "Excellent oral and written communication skills." Duh.
- "Organized and attentive to detail." Duh.
- "Strong interests and expert capabilities in the design and development of engaging user experiences are a must." Marketing-speak.
- "<Our UX Designer> must be a motivated, one-step-ahead

39

kind of thinker, and someone who is able to collaborate with other team members." Duh.

- "We're looking for a creative, passionate, and detail-oriented <UX Designer>." Duh.
- "A macro and micro-thinker who can just as easily zoom out to look at the whole and zoom in to be detail-oriented." Marketing-speak.
- "Highly sensitized to the user experience with finely tuned design sensibilities." Huh?
- "<Company name> is looking for a Head of User Experience, who is passionate, creative and an out-of-the-box RockStar UXer." Sigh.
- "Looking for a design rockstar; passionate and driven, one who thrives in a cross-functional and vibrant team environment spread across continents, is comfortable engaging with end users, and loves creating delightful experiences." Mic drop.

BEYOND THE GENERAL HIGH-LEVEL SKILLS

"Help perform pre- and post-development usability testing to validate business needs and user goals"

Your level of involvement here will depend on whether you're going to operate more as a generalist/UX team of one or if you're going to be part of a larger UX team with specialized roles. Some companies have user researchers/usability engineers who focus exclusively on user research tasks and usability testing, then share what they've learned with the rest of the team.

"Experience in Lean, Agile or Iterative UXD environments"

The two most common approaches to product development are

Waterfall and Agile (or a hybrid of both, sometimes jokingly referred to as "wagile" or "agile-fall").

In Waterfall, each step of the project is a distinct, different phase, and approval of one phase is needed before the next phase begins. Waterfall favors detailed documentation and formal sign-offs.

Agile, on the other hand, is an iterative, fluid approach, where phases can run alongside each other. Agile focuses on collaboration and the reduction of documentation and formal sign-offs (which dovetails into the Lean UX movement). Most companies are following the Agile methodology these days. In a 2017 UXPin survey, 93% of the 3,157 respondents said their companies followed an Agile or hybrid process. So a lot of companies are starting to include "knowledge of Agile" in their job descriptions.

This is tricky because it's not your fault if the place you work for now doesn't follow the Agile methodology. It's not like you can go off and get a bunch of Agile experience on your own, and honestly it's not that hard to acclimate to Agile (the user-centered design process is already iterative, so we're used to that). As UXers, we often work on the periphery of Agile, versus embedded inside development "scrum" teams, and every company integrates UX into their Agile process differently.

If you have zero Agile experience but the job posting is asking for it, you can take a couple of Agile classes or tutorials online and internalize some of the concepts and popular terminology (like scrum, sprints, standups, backlog, etc.), then you can at least say that you are "familiar with" Agile and speak to it if comes up during an interview.

HTML, CSS, AND JAVASCRIPT
There are two ways hiring managers usually phrase this:

41

- *"Knowledge of JavaScript, HTML, CSS, and other front-end technologies."* When I read this, I think, "As a designer, I should understand what their limitations are, and can have an intelligent conversation about them with a developer." This is how much a UX designer should be expected to know about HTML, CSS, etc.
- *"Comfortable translating mockups to HTML, CSS, and JavaScript."* This isn't a UX designer, this is a unicorn.

VISUAL DESIGN KNOWLEDGE

Similar to the HTML/CSS/JavaScript requirements, you'll usually see visual design skills mentioned in a few different ways:

1. *"The ability to work with a visual system. You won't need full-stack design chops or illustration abilities, but you can work effectively within a strong and established design system and design your own brand compliant UIs."* When I see this, I think, "Ok, great, they have a style guide and I can use those guidelines to help me design my wireframes and prototypes." Many of my prototypes incorporate the brand's colors, fonts, button styles, headers, etc. into them. They aren't pixel-perfect and I don't do them in Adobe-anything (I do all the styling right in Axure), but they give everybody a good idea of what the end result should look like.

2. *"Design and prototype innovative and visually stunning interfaces that reflect <Company name>'s brand and vision."* This is a red flag. Most prototypes don't need to be "visually stunning" unless they are production-quality visual designs. This sounds like they're expecting you to create prototypes and the final visual design.

3. *"Experience designing high-quality graphic assets in Sketch, Illustrator, Photoshop."* This isn't a UX designer, this is a visual designer (or a unicorn).

TOOLS
Prototyping
Here is my favorite type of requirement to see because it shows that the company understands that there is no one "right" tool to use for wireframes and prototypes: *"You have experience with interaction design analysis and prototyping tools (Axure, Sketch, Balsamiq, etc.)"*

Graphics
Many of the job postings these days also require Adobe Creative Suite, but I don't know why. Creative Suite was actually retired in 2016 (CS6 was the last version) and replaced by Creative Cloud, so I'm not even sure what Adobe applications the hiring managers are asking for as part of "Creative Suite."

The CS6 "Design Standard" package came with Photoshop, Illustrator, InDesign, and Acrobat Pro. As a UX designer, the only Adobe product I've ever needed was Photoshop. And I don't use it to create a lot of original graphics, I use it to take screenshots, crop graphics and photos (to import into my prototypes), identify colors and fonts on websites, and tweak colors on things like icons.

Sometimes companies narrow things down too much. Tools are easy – you can take some online classes and teach yourself a tool quickly. What's more important is that you're a good designer... that's tool independent. Don't get discouraged if companies weed you out based on overly-specific skills. Just move on.

Red flags:
If companies put things like this into their job description, tread carefully:
 • *"The desire to learn and see obstacles as opportunities is a must. It's not easy to work here, but it's never boring."*

- *"High tolerance for ambiguity matched only by your desire to organize it"*
- *"Collaborate with teams to review and ensure difficult UX features can be executed accurately against design concepts"*

The ability to do all of these things (thrive in ambiguity, ensure difficult features are executed accurately, etc.) is critical – the red flag is that they actually included it in their job description. At least they're being honest, I guess. I'd make a note of anything that rings little warning bells and make sure you investigate it (or ask about it directly) during the interview process.

Also beware of the job description that looks like it's asking for too much (back to the unicorn). Even if you have all those skills, it's probably more work than one person can handle.

[5]

How to Get More Experience

This chapter isn't just geared toward new UXers. If you're a senior-level UXer who's ready for a new job challenge, you may feel like your portfolio is a little thin (especially if you've been working on the same project for years) and that you're out of the loop when it comes to some of these new design tools.

Everything changes so fast in our industry, it's hard to keep up even if you're trying to stay on top of things.

Speak the Language

If you want to get into UX, you need to be comfortable speaking UXese. And you need to sound like a real UXer, not a poser. I want you to be able to walk into any interview situation and understand the questions they're asking you and be able to speak to it all naturally and confidently.

You do not need to be a member of some secret club to learn how to do this. You just need to immerse yourself in UX, using some of the suggestions in this chapter. Take a few classes, watch a few videos, read some books and blogs. Go to some Meetups, where you can practice talking to other UXers.

Study the user-centered design process and the different activities and deliverables that fall under each step. Understand what the different UX roles are and what they produce and how they relate to each other.

Educate Yourself

There are so many great resources out there, and most of them are inexpensive and can be done from home.

LYNDA.COM

Lynda.com, which was recently bought by LinkedIn, has been around for 20 years and has thousands of high-quality online classes that focus primarily on technical and creative skills. I just did a search on "UX" and got 1,713 results. They have in-depth classes on tools like Sketch, InVision, and Axure and how-to classes for pretty much any UX topic you can think of (and also peripheral topics like Agile software development).

Although Lynda.com usually costs $19.99 a month (after a free 30-day trial…you could learn a lot in 30 days…just sayin'), many public libraries offer free access to it through their websites. Search your local library's website (*not* the book catalog) for Lynda.com. If they offer it, you can log in using your library card # and password (the first time you log in you'll need to create a profile). It's a little kluge to access but worth the trouble.

UIE'S ALL YOU CAN LEARN

All You Can Learn (aycl.uie.com), which is part of usability expert Jared Spool's companies User Interface Engineering (UIE) and Center Centre, is an ongoing series of recorded talks and presentations given by high-profile UXers for other UXers. All You Can Learn includes on-stage talks from UX conferences as well as online presentations ranging from 30-90 minutes long on all sorts of UX-related topics. I enjoy the content because the speakers/presenters know their stuff (most have written UX books and have been in the industry a long time). You feel like an insider when you listen to them. If you're new to UX, listening to them can help you internalize a lot of the UX terminology and user-centered design process.

All You Can Learn costs $29 a month so I call it "All You Can Learn in a Month." I've renewed it and canceled it several times over the past few years to get caught up with the latest presentations.

UDEMY

Udemy (udemy.com) is an online learning website similar to Lynda.com. There is a lot of junk on Udemy (anybody can publish anything they want as long as the video/sound quality passes Udemy's standards) but there are a few good UX classes, including a comprehensive one from UK usability consultant David Travis, called "User Experience (UX): The Ultimate Guide to Usability and UX."

Travis also has a very active Facebook group where past and present students of his class can exchange ideas and ask questions. The class is geared toward beginners and includes some good design exercises.

Don't ever pay full price for anything on Udemy. They have big sales all the time.

LOCAL MEETUPS

We have an active UX Meetup community in the Denver/Boulder area, including several groups with over 1,500 members each. Most of the groups have monthly happy hours, plus regular meetings held at local UX agencies or schools like General Assembly. Most meetings are built around a group design exercise or a presentation, and they get lots of good guest speakers.

Some recent presentations from Meetups near me included:
- UX Portfolio Review
- Sketch Advanced Tips & Tricks Workshop
- Building a Seat at the Table: Promoting User-centered Designs with Stakeholders
- Panel Discussion: Hiring for UX
- Usability Testing Workshop
- Design Studio Workshop w/Boulder County
- UX Portfolios: Design for Your User (the Hiring Manager and Recruiter)

Meetups are a good place to learn, network, and meet other local UXers. It's also a great way to find out about local job openings. And who knows, maybe you'll sit next to the hiring manager at one of the happy hours.

LOCAL DESIGN SCHOOLS

Some people (myself included) like to learn in person. For me, it's the ultimate accountability. If I'm shelling out some money and driving somewhere to spend all day in a classroom, I'm going to get everything I can out of it and leave brain-dead with pages of notes.

Going somewhere in person also means that I can't distract myself at home with other things like housework, Facebook, dogs, etc. That day is set aside to learn and that's it.

Use Google to search for UX classes in your area. You'll probably find day-long workshops, week-long certificate classes, and longer "bootcamp" classes that can span several weeks or months (many schools offer part-time hours and/or evening and weekend hours so you can take these classes while working a full-time job). You might even be able to talk your current company into paying for the class.

Most in-person certificate courses and bootcamps focus on creating a UX project that you can include in your portfolio. These classes are usually very collaborative, allowing you to leverage the experience of your instructor and the skills of all the other students (visual designers, writers, programmers, marketing people, business people, etc.) to help you with your project.

BOOKS

There are so many great UX books out there. I'll include a list of my favorites in the Resources section at the end of this book (and on my website at lisamurnan.com/resources).

In general, most of the O'Reilly books (the ones with the animal illustrations and purple accent colors on the cover) are great, and so are the Rosenfeld Media books. The authors are all very experienced solid UXers writing for other UXers.

Steve Krug's *Don't Make Me Think* is a must-read classic. Start with that.

ARTICLES/BLOGS

My favorite place to read articles about UX is on Medium. It's like a blog, but with lots of authors gathered in one place. There are so many current UX-related topics featured on there and the comments sections are often as thought-provoking and entertaining as the articles themselves.

I also subscribe to Nielsen Norman Group's email newsletter. They publish an article or two a week about usability-related issues and the articles are always full of great statistics and examples. You can subscribe (or just read the articles online) at nngroup.com.

OTHER UX DESIGNERS' DELIVERABLES

A Google search for "UX Deliverables" will yield over a million results – of course, you'll have to separate the wheat from the chaff, but studying other designers' deliverables (both good and bad) will teach you a lot.

First, you'll see that everybody creates their deliverables a little differently and that's okay, as long as the deliverable conveys what it needs to for its target user. Second, you can see how other designers think, and learn from their thought processes. Third, you can identify aspects of their deliverables that you like and borrow them to use in your own deliverables.

You can do the same thing with other designers' online portfolios. Why did they make the design decisions they made? What types of deliverables did they use in each of their projects, and what did they do to understand their users' goals/needs?

One online portfolio I am fascinated with is interaction designer Simon Pan's (simonpan.com). Although his case studies are very long (his Uber case study was 65 screens long on my 1920 x 1080 display), they are interesting as hell to read and full of insights, user research photos, screenshots, and UX strategy. He discusses his process in exquisite detail – if you want to learn about how to apply the user-centered design process to real projects, read his case studies.

Get Hands-On Experience

This is often the big Catch-22. You need more experience to be considered for the jobs you want, but you can't get the experience without experience.

Here are a few ways to work more UX into your life so that you can acquire the skills you need and add more projects to your portfolio.

START INCORPORATING UX-RELATED TASKS AT YOUR CURRENT JOB

Many of you are stuck in jobs that don't make you happy. You want to get out of that job ASAP. I get it. But you can use your current job to get resume-worthy UX experience in the meantime.

You don't even need to get your manager's permission to do it, and you'll probably end up making whatever project you're working on better at the same time.

You can:
- Do lots and lots of user research for your current project/product and its target audience.
- Create personas and user scenarios based on this research.
- Conduct contextual interviews (basically talking to people 1-on-1, either on the phone while you're screen sharing or at their desk where you can watch them work) as part of your research.
- Map out some task flows or user flows to help define how a user will move through the screens of your product to accomplish something.
- Create a customer journey map by figuring out the different touchpoints a customer has with your company/product (from sales to onboarding to support, etc.), identifying areas of friction, then coming up with recommendations for how to remove that friction from the user experience.
- Sketch design ideas and even mock them up in something non-threatening (to others) like Balsamiq. (Balsamiq's output looks very sketch-like, versus some of the other design tools that can look pixel-perfect). The product managers at my company recently started using Balsamiq to help them think through business requirements for their products. They use their wireframes to get everybody on the same page with their

vision. Then they work with the UX team to take their design ideas to the next level.

- Conduct guerilla usability testing (which might mean walking over to somebody's desk with your laptop or a few printouts and asking them what they think about something you're working on).
- Learn Google Analytics or some other tool that will come in handy for your next job.

And boom, now you're able to add bullet points to your resume for each of these skills. Maybe your company will even pay for you to attend a UX class or conference.

TAKE A "STEPPING STONE" JOB

If your current job offers no opportunity for learning/experimenting, another approach is to take a job that's somewhere in between your current job and your UX dream job and use that in-between job to get the skills, experience, and perhaps even job title you need to actually land your dream job.

When I mention this option to my students I'm usually met with several rows of sour faces staring back at me. Again, I get it. You want to get into your UX dream job as soon as possible and the idea of putting it off for another year or two for some in-between job is excruciating and unacceptable (and to be honest, that would be my reaction as well). But for some people, it's the perfect solution.

FIND FREELANCE PROJECTS TO WORK ON

Look for websites you can redesign or create from scratch. Friends and family members may have businesses or hobbies that need a website. Organizations you're associated with (clubs, church, PTA, etc.), and local nonprofits may need your UX help as well.

Don't get hung up on making money at this point. Your goal is to get more experience and build up your portfolio. If people are willing to pay you, great, but don't walk away from a project if it can provide you with crucial experience. Another option is to trade time or services. Once I helped a friend design a website for her hair salon and for every hour I put in on her website she credited me an hour of her time at the salon.

When you work on small websites for family and friends you'll often get the opportunity to use tools like WordPress and Google Analytics, and to consult with visual designers or developers. This is all great experience.

Another place to look for design work is in programmer Meetup groups. They often participate in group projects or Hackathons and love to have UX help on their projects.

Document everything you do along the way. It's easy to discard your sketches or whiteboard drawings or Post-it Note process flows and move right into prototyping and designing, but take photos and screenshots as you go so that you can add this documentation to your portfolio.

Also, create deliverables even when nobody asks for them. If your uncle has a business and wants your help with a website, he's not going to be asking you for things like personas, user scenarios, task flows, etc., but take the time to create these for your own experience and to add to your portfolio. If you're redesigning your dog club's website from 2004, run your own card sorting exercise with several target users (club members) and document the results.

Solve your own problem. Is there something that drives you crazy and you have an idea for an app or website that would fix it?

Is there an existing website or app out there with serious usability issues that you'd love to fix (*cough* Snapchat *cough, cough*)? Design it and document it.

However, I want to go on the record to say that this approach is my least favorite of all the ideas I've mentioned so far, because you don't have access to the same business goals, user research, constraints, etc. that the product's original designers had. You can't tell a story about redesigning a website/app like this the way you could with a project where you're actually interacting with a client, end users, stakeholders, etc., and coming up with a design solution from scratch.

Any freelance or personal project can be used in a portfolio if you use it to show how you understand and embrace the UX process, and include high-quality examples of your work. (And let's be honest…a lot of the UX job postings try to sound glamorous but they're really looking for someone to design a customer service website for a phone company, or software for roofing/gutter manufacturers, or a life insurance website…so don't let them make you feel stupid about anything in your portfolio. We can't all work for Google or Facebook.)

LAND AN INTERNSHIP

I'm including internships because it would be remiss of me not to, but they are hard to come by and often require candidates to be currently enrolled in college and working toward a UX-related degree. Most of the internship opportunities are located in San Francisco or one of the other big tech hubs.

Interns generally don't work for free – the salaries I saw during my research were on the low end of the junior designer range.

TEST OTHER PEOPLE'S WEBSITES

You can sign up to be a usability tester with UserTesting (usert-esting.com) and earn money while getting the inside scoop on what companies are doing from a UX standpoint.

UserTesting is basically the middle man between companies who want something tested (like their existing website/app, a work in progress, or even a competitor's website) and pre-screened usability test participants.

As a tester, you get to click around on websites or apps, complete a set of tasks while thinking out loud, and get paid for it. You provide feedback in the form of a 20-minute screen-capture video (your face won't be on video, so you can drink wine in your pajamas during the test if you want), and you make $10 per test, which UserTesting deposits right into your PayPal account. Starbucks money!

Tools

On one hand, it's a good idea to keep up with the newest tools (like Sketch & InVision right now). On the other hand, it's a pain to learn new design software every couple of years. And you might not be able to use the latest and greatest at work, so it's difficult to get practical experience with a new tool. For example, Sketch is only available for Mac right now, and my company only uses PCs, so I can't even download Sketch to practice with it at work. Plus my company just invested in several Axure licenses a couple of years ago, and everybody is happy with the Axure wireframes/prototypes that we produce. Why would they want to invest in something new right now?

And it really doesn't matter that much *what* you use to convey and present your ideas as long as whatever tool you use works. The tools and technology change all the time, but the output doesn't.

It does matter from a practicality standpoint if the company you work for or want to work for has a certain tool that it uses and expects all its UX designers to know and use. But once you know one design tool really well, it's pretty easy to pick up new ones. It's sort of like knowing Microsoft PowerPoint then switching to Google Slides or Keynote.

In my 23 years of designing user experiences, here are the tools that I find indispensable, that I use daily:

- Wireframing/prototyping software, like Axure (before Axure I used Visio, before that Dreamweaver, before that HTML).
- Adobe Photoshop (or anything that will let you take screenshots and crop/edit images).

That's pretty much it. Sometimes I need to write something, so I use Word or Google Docs. Sometimes I need to create a presentation, so I use PowerPoint. Chrome is my browser of choice. I use tools like Skype, Jira, Confluence, Trello, Slack, etc., based on what projects I'm working on and how that particular team chooses to communicate. The tools change but the work doesn't.

[6]

STAR Approach

Behavioral interviews are the big thing these days. Google, who was notorious for asking crazy brainteaser questions and requesting job candidates' college GPAs (even when they were 20 years out of school), switched their approach to behavioral questions because they found (through analyzing data as only Google can) that behavioral questions were a much better way of assessing whether a candidate would be a good fit or not.

Laszlo Bock from Google told the *New York Times*, "The interesting thing about the behavioral interview is that when you ask somebody to speak to their own experience, and you drill into that, you get two kinds of information. One is you get to see how they actually interacted in a real-world situation, and the valuable 'meta' information you get about the candidate is a sense of what they consider to be difficult."

Behavioral questions, which we'll cover more in Chapters 12 and 13, usually start with "Tell me about a time when…" and ask you to relay a story about when you failed, struggled, or disagreed with someone. Good times, right?

Since you'll already be stressed out because you're in an interview and you have no idea what sort of angst from your past they're going to ask you to dredge up, it helps to have a secret weapon you can use to quickly collect your thoughts and structure a coherent answer to any question.

Enter STAR.

STAR stands for Situation, Task, Actions, Results. It is a great way to structure a story quickly.

SITUATION: Setting the scene with details about the company, the project, and the timeframe.

TASK: What was your role on the project or in the particular situation?

ACTIONS: What were the steps you took and what was your thought process during each step?

RESULTS: What was the outcome of the situation, and what did you learn from the experience?

HERE'S AN EXAMPLE.

Question: Tell me about a time when you faced a major obstacle at work?

STAR Answer: First, set up the Situation/Task.

My first contract with ABC Company was in 2011 and I was brought in as the UX Lead for the LemonTree website.

The product owner was a guy named Ted, and everybody warned me about how difficult he was to work with. There were stories about my manager getting into legendary shouting matches with him during meetings and the other UX people on the team made little comments to me about how he was "challenging." They all seemed very happy not to be me.

I was dreading the whole thing.

Next, talk about Actions.

I decided right then that I was not going to fall into the same sort of power-struggle trap that others had fallen into. I had been down that road in the past and it never went well.

First, I went out of my way to collaborate with him and listen to his ideas (which were actually really good) and to share my work with him as I was going.

Second, I always ran things past him before a review meeting with UX management or his manager or other executives so that he wasn't taken by surprise in front of other people. This meant by the time I showed design ideas in meetings, he had already seen them and weighed in on them and even contributed to them, so we became a united front in review calls, and he would usually defend the design versus shooting it down. If he did have issues with the design, he would state them very respectfully and constructively.

Third, I never threw him under the bus. If I had issues or concerns about anything, I reached out to him and chatted about them privately before they became a bigger issue.

Then, talk about Results.

We ended up developing a great relationship, and he talked me up to all the guys on the business side of things and introduced me to them and trusted me to set up meetings and collaborate with them without him. He knew I'd keep him posted on my progress and that I'd let him know if I had any questions.

The screens we designed always tested great in usability tests and went through major executive reviews with flying colors, and I believe it's because the team was so open and collaborative.

My first contract ended at ABC in 2012, but in 2013 they called me back and asked if I wanted to take on another project, this time for the OrangeCandy product line. And guess who was the product owner? Ted. He had asked to

work with me specifically. And once again we designed some great stuff
that I was really proud of.

This may look like a long answer but it goes by quickly when
you're telling the story.

You can use the STAR approach to answer any situational-type
interview question and also to structure the case studies in your
portfolio.

[7]

Resume

I recently reviewed the resume of someone who wanted to switch from product management to a career in UX design. Although he had all the right jargon in there, the whole thing rang hollow. It was just so generic. It read like a series of job description bullet points versus a summary of his experience and accomplishments. I imagined a hiring manager picking it up, glancing at it, then putting it in the circular file.

You need to make your resume stand out from the generic UX resumes. This is especially true at the junior level, when you're trying to prove that you do indeed know what you're doing. Some UX designers make the mistake of jazzing up their resumes with cartoon images of their faces, big swoops of color, and giant fonts. This is not the way you want to stand out. Stand out with the *quality of your content*.

Focus on your accomplishments versus your duties. This can be hard for a UXer – we often don't have impressive numbers to throw around like someone in sales or product management ("increased sales by $5M in one year!"), so we need to get more creative with it.

Hiring Manager Alison Green, who runs the popular blog *Ask a Manager*, gives the following helpful advice:

"To get at this stuff, try asking yourself: What did you accomplish in this job that someone else might not have? Did you make improvements or do something that got better results than your employer had been getting before? If you were asked what made you really great at your job, what would you say? What might your boss or coworkers have said made you really great? Somewhere in there are qualitative accomplishments – and, ideally, a track record of getting things done."

Focus on micro-accomplishments versus macro-accomplishments. If you can't say that your design solutions were responsible for an x% increase in conversions, talk instead about how your user research uncovered some interesting trends that the team wasn't previously aware of, or how you introduced a new way of brainstorming on the team that resulted in a lot more design ideas up front. Get specific.

A bullet point like "Conducted interviews with current customers to uncover pain points/likes" doesn't say much of anything. We don't even know if you were any good at it. But if you say something like, "Conducted contextual interviews with security analysts, resulting in important observations about their work environment that directly influenced our design," you're painting a picture of why what you do matters.

Here's an example from my own resume.

I had: "Collaborate with product management and engineering to define and design innovative user interfaces and user experience solutions for Company A's web and mobile applications." Anybody reading this would say, "Well, duh. That's what UX designers do."

I replaced that sentence with these three sentences: "Tackle challenging design problems in a highly complex environment.

Redesign business-critical web apps used by security analysts in Company A's Counter Threat Operations Centers to investigate and process security events faster for clients. Collaborate with product management and Counter Threat Unit on next-gen design for the SaaS-delivered <Product Name> portal."

I know the wording isn't perfect, but the new sentences convey that I design complex, business-critical applications that help employees do their jobs faster. I even managed to work the word "SaaS" in there (a buzzword on so many job postings these days). This rewrite is so much better than the original generic blah blah blah bullet point.

Here's another example:

Before: "Led UX design on many digital projects including Company B's authenticated customer portal." *Yawn.*

After: "Led UX design on many digital projects including Company B's authenticated customer portal, which improved the user experience for millions of customers."

I didn't have any specific metrics, but I *know* it was better than it was before, and the "millions of customers" detail was important, it showed that my work impacted a lot of people.

One more:

Before: "Communicated solution approach through user flows, site maps, and wireframes and prototypes." *Boring.*

After: "Worked collaboratively with user researchers, content strategists, and visual designers to create innovative design solutions. Our mortgage app, which boiled the whole mortgage loan process down into four simple steps, got rave reviews from Mortgage and eCommerce executives. The head of eCommerce even traveled in person to present the design to Company C's CEO." Can you tell how much more engaged and invested I sound? Doesn't it sound so much more *real*?

Ok, now you try. Don't feel like you have to change every single bullet point in your resume. Focus on your most recent position, plus at least one bullet point from each past job. Show that you've accomplished something everywhere you've worked.

PAST NON-UX JOBS AND TRANSFERABLE SKILLS

If you are switching from a career in sales or product management or development or whatever to one in UX, do not panic and hide all your past jobs and create a "functional" resume that just lists out your skills and whatever UX experience you have.

Most hiring managers hate functional resumes because they make it look like you're hiding something from your work experience. Your resume should always include a chronological job history.

Besides, those past jobs serve as a track record of your accomplishments and experience, and prove you are a professional that should be taken seriously. And there are probably some transferable skills that you can highlight in those job descriptions.

Maybe you did some focus groups or surveys or market research or competitive research (all align with user research), or print design or game design (align with information architecture, interaction design, and visual design), or front-end development with CSS/HTML/JavaScript (align with interaction design), or data analytics (align with usability testing). Maybe you talked to customers regularly in a sales or customer support job, and you passed along their feature requests and pain points to product management. Build a bridge between these skills and UX skills.

ATS

Most companies today use an Applicant Tracking System (ATS) to screen and score candidates' resumes. ATSs are just searchable HR databases that help recruiters and hiring managers sift through large pools of applicants quickly. It's not unusual for one job posting to get 200-300 applications since it's so easy for people to apply online these days with tools like LinkedIn's "Easy Apply."

When you apply for a job online and attach or copy/paste your resume (or send a stored copy of it through LinkedIn or Monster or Indeed), it is probably going into an ATS. A candidate profile is created for you at that point, and all your information is parsed into categories (like Experience, Education, Skills, etc.) and goes into that profile.

Recruiters and hiring managers can search their ATS by keyword. Keywords are weighted based on the specific job description. This means you're going to need to customize your resume for every job you apply for. Oh my god, *no*, you say. What a huge pain in the ass! Yes, it is. Bye bye, Easy Apply.

DECONSTRUCTING KEYWORDS

I just went onto LinkedIn and typed "UX Designer" into the Jobs search bar, printed out the first six matches, and highlighted the relevant keywords.

One job description said "interactive design" and another said "interaction design." One said "User Experience Testing" and another said "usability testing." One said "S.A.A.S." and another said "SaaS." One said "user-centered design" and another said "User Centric Design." Some spelled it "wireframe," others spelled it "wire-frame." Two said "Adobe Creative Suite" while others just listed out the individual programs, like "Adobe

Illustrator" or just "Illustrator." One even had "Abode Illustrator." It's enough to boggle the mind, isn't it?

I'm not sure how smart ATSs are, plus the functionality varies from software to software (Taleo's capabilities are different from Bullhorn's, for example), so I don't know if they understand that "wire-framing" is the same thing as "wireframing" or "S.A.A.S." is the same thing as "SaaS." I just can't bring myself to intentionally spell words wrong in my resume to match a job posting, so I'm going to spell them correctly and hope for the best. I gotta think a company will miss out on a lot of other great candidates, too, when the recruiter types "Abode Illustrator" into the search box. And do I even want to be a designer at a company that can't spell Adobe?

Anyway, if the job posting is referring to an important job requirement in a certain way, mirror that in your resume where you can. You don't need to focus on every word, just the words and phrases you think they're going to be searching on. For example, I wouldn't bother trying to figure out how to incorporate "outstanding communicator" or "rockstar" into my resume but I would make sure I included industry-specific keywords that were in the job posting, like "prototypes," "usability testing," "wireframes," "Sketch," "InVision," and "Agile." Use exact keywords, down to the tense (i.e. if the job description says "wireframes," use that versus "wireframing" or "wireframed").

A note about tools, since I just mentioned Sketch and InVision. My wireframing/prototyping tool of choice is Axure. I've used it for years and I love it. But I know enough about Sketch and InVision to be dangerous, precisely so I can include them on my resume. If I needed to get up to speed on Sketch and/or InVision quickly in order to start a new job, I have no doubt I could crank through some YouTube tutorials and a Lynda.com class or two and know enough to start working proficiently in them. I might not know all the nuances of how to collaborate with other team members using them, but I could pick that up quickly enough.

I'm telling you this because almost every job posting I looked at during my research specifically asked for Sketch. They often worded it as, "Proficient with wireframing tools such as Sketch or Balsamiq," which technically would also include Axure, but if somebody is putting a keyword into the ATS they're going to put in Sketch, not Axure.

It's also okay to edit your job title as long as the roles are essentially the same and you're not giving yourself a promotion. For example, in my current job my official title is Principal UI Engineer, but I tacked on "UX Designer" because that's really what I do. It's not my fault that my company wants to give everybody in Engineering an engineering title. If your title is "Interaction Designer" or "Information Architect" and all the jobs you're applying for are "UX Designer," consider changing your title on your resume, or calling yourself a UX Designer in your Summary.

That being said, if you are a developer who is also doing some front-end coding and dabbling in UI/UX stuff because there's no UX designer assigned to your project, it is not okay to change your job title to "UX Designer." But you should absolutely include the UX work you're doing in the bullet points under your job title.

One easy way to customize your resume quickly for individual job postings is to include a skills section and add/delete/rephrase the relevant keywords there. But according to ATS experts, the content inside each job description is weighted higher than skills listed in a separate skills section. And your most recent work experience is weighted the highest, so if there's a way for you to legitimately work those keywords into your current job description, do it.

It could be as simple as rewriting your bullet points from something like this:

"Conduct user research, perform heuristic reviews, create wireframes and prototypes, create visual design assets, study metrics to understand user behavior."

To this (changes are highlighted in bold):

"Conduct user research, perform heuristic reviews, create wireframes and prototypes **in Axure**, create visual design assets **in Adobe Photoshop**, study **Google Analytics** metrics to understand user behavior."

When you're trying to decide which keywords to use in your resume, choose based on this order:
1. The hiring employer's keywords
2. UX industry standard keywords
3. Your current/most recent employer's keywords.

My friend told me a story at lunch the other day about how her husband (we'll call him "Brian") has become a master at manipulating his resume for the ATS. Brian, who was laid off from his IT job a few months ago, starting using a web app called Jobscan (jobscan.co) to compare his resume with job descriptions and get a "match rate" score (based on keywords, job title, etc.)

As Brian started customizing his resumes to match the job desciptions more and more (with his goal being a match rate of 80% or higher), he started getting an increasing number of inquiries from recruiters who wanted to set up interviews, even with companies he had no previous connection with. My friend said the results have been amazing, and Brian has even started doing it for her resume as well (with the same results). I have no affiliation with

Jobscan, but it sounds like it's worth checking out (or maybe we should all go straight to Brian!).

Don't try to trick the system by adding the same keyword over and over again in white text. (Webmasters used to do that a long time ago to rank their pages higher in the search engines, before Google took all the fun out of it. We'd put a huge chunk of keywords down at the bottom of the web page and make the text color the same as the background color so that site visitors couldn't see it. Some webmasters would even include totally irrelevant keywords like "sex" just to get their site to show up in the search results!). Some ATSs convert everything in your resume to plain black text and if that happens, you're busted, cheater.

Also, I'd save a copy of every resume you submit (and the corresponding job description) so that you can keep track of how you worded everything.

FORMATTING THE ATS-FRIENDLY RESUME

I can't tell you how painful this part has been for me. I'm on my fourth iteration of the ATS-friendly resume because it has been so hard for me to remove all the formatting that would make it easier for people to read.

Although ATSs are getting more and more sophisticated, I've decided to go hardcore simple with this. First, because a person is not going to see this version of my resume, so it doesn't need to look pretty. Second, because the end user is a robot. And as UXers aren't we always taught to design for our users? Third, because the simpler the design, the easier it will be to customize for each job posting.

ATS ROBOT – "ROBOT"	
"Robot is on-line."	
Overview	• There are hundreds of ATS platforms on the market, the most popular being Taleo, Homegrown, Jobvite, iCims, and Greenhouse Software. • Over 50% of employers (and 90% of large companies) are using ATSs, which represents 70-80% of job ads. • Major job sites, like Indeed, LinkedIn, and Monster, integrate with ATSs on the backend.
Goals	• Parse out data from resumes into logical groupings • Search data and and provide ranked results based on keywords entered • Destroy Robinson family
Pain Points	When people spell "Adobe" wrong
UX Knowledge	n/a
Interaction with You	• Sucks your carefully crafted resume into its system and dices it up however it wants

ATSs have the easiest time parsing plain text or Microsoft Word files, so create your resume in Word if you can. ATS software companies claim that they can parse PDFs just fine now (there were issues in the past), but why risk it if you don't have to? If you do use a program like Adobe InDesign to create your resume and have to save it out as a PDF, make sure that you can copy/

paste the text from your resume into a text editor like TextPad or Notepad before you submit it anywhere.

My friend Julie told me a funny (but slightly terrifying) story about a friend who was baffled because she had been applying for jobs and hearing absolutely nothing back. When Julie reviewed her friend's resume, she discovered that it had been made in Photoshop, exported as an image, then saved as a PDF, which flattened everything and made it impossible for any ATS to scan. Don't do that.

Your ATS resume should have no document headers or footers (like in Word). No fancy fonts (I use Arial). No colors. No tables. No columns. No horizontal lines separating sections.

Bullets are a-ok, and I also use bold for section headers just in case it helps the system recognize them as headers.Instead of adding extra space or aligning certain elements to the right (like the start/end dates), just stack the content like this:

Work Experience
Company Name
Denver, CO
UX Designer
11/2014 - Present
• Bullet point one
• Bullet point two
• Etc.

Use standard resume headings, like "Work Experience" and "Education" so that the ATS knows how to parse out your resume content. My resume has the following sections, in this order:

- Summary
- Work Experience
- Education
- Skills

Note that the first section is a *summary*, not an *objective*. A Summary is a nice sentence or two about who you are and what you do, while an Objective is a sentence or two about what you *want* to do. Employers want to know what you can do for them (not what you want to do), and if you're qualified for the job.

The Pretty Resume
Yay! Now you can take all the content from the robot resume and make it look nice for a human being again.

Your pretty resume should be clean and, well, pretty, but not over the top. It doesn't need to show off all your mad UX skillzzz – that's what your portfolio is for. While researching resumes for this book, I actually saw one where a UX designer put a giant pink unicorn graphic as a design element at the top of the page. Please don't do that. You'll stand out, for sure, but not in the right way.

I recently talked with a recruiter about resume formats and she said that she appreciated resumes that were visually pleasing and easy to scan. "Ironically," she said, "sometimes the UX resumes are the hardest to navigate." She said that charts that tried to visually show various skills and expertise were particularly confusing, and she recommended that candidates just provide a list of skills instead. She also said that she was seeing a lot more photos on resumes these days (especially from millennials), although photos "used to be a big no-no." She said she just overlooks the photos now. (The way I interpret that is that including a photo on your resume isn't doing a bit of good, and may even be hurting your chances.)

My pretty resume has a simple layout and minimal formatting. Since I'm old, I have a lot of content to cram on there, so I use the traditional resume format where the content takes up the whole width of the page and flows in sections from top to bottom. I've seen some resumes that divide the page up into two vertical columns (in a 2/3 to 1/3 ratio) – one column for job experience and the other for education information and lists of things like skills. This format is great for somebody who has less experience and needs to fill the page a bit.

I use a sans-serif font for the headers (including my name and contact info at the top) and a serif font for the body content. I use one accent color (blue) and it's only for my name and the headers (Summary, Work Experience, etc.). The blue helps the headers pop out on the page without being too distracting.

I would only create customized versions of your pretty resume on a need-to-have basis – you won't need one unless you make it past the ATS and get to talk to a real person. They may ask you to email them a copy, or if you get in for an interview you'll want to bring printouts of your resume to hand out.

Make sure there are no discrepancies between the content in this resume and the ATS-friendly resume you already submitted.

A Note About LinkedIn

Your LinkedIn profile is essentially your third resume, but it's even better because you can use their "Summary" area to write an engaging bio, include links to media (websites, videos, etc.), and talk about any volunteer work you're involved with.

LinkedIn also has a "Recommendations" section where people can endorse you. You can't fit all that stuff on a traditional resume!

These days, I get contacted by recruiters on LinkedIn all the time. I noticed a big increase in recruiters viewing my profile and messaging me after I did several things:

1. Turned on that little beacon letting recruiters know I was open to hearing about opportunities (on your profile page's Dashboard under "Career Interests").

2. Updated my "Experience" section with all my jobs and consulting work, and linked to current and former employers who had a page on LinkedIn so that their company logos appeared next to my job descriptions.

3. Rewrote my job descriptions so that they focused more on my accomplishments, and replaced the original job description language with more modern terminology from today's job postings.

4. Took the time to craft a good summary, and at the bottom of the summary I created sections for "Expertise" and "Tools" and listed out every skill I had that matched the common ones I was seeing in all the UX job postings.

5. Added all my relevant skills to the "Featured Skills & Endorsements" section. Even though skill endorsements from your network aren't actively promoted/solicited by LinkedIn anymore, adding skills to that section helps recruiters find you in searches.

Recruiters are searching for candidates on LinkedIn the same way they are searching through an ATS. They are plugging in keywords and locations and seeing who pops up in the search results. Obviously, your LinkedIn profile has to be a little bit generic, because you have no idea who is going to look at it, but be sure to populate your profile with all the right UX keywords and phrases and make sure every section is filled out.

BULLET POINTS

Although I include bullet points in the resumes I design in Word (the ATS and pretty versions), bullet points look junky on LinkedIn. LinkedIn doesn't let you bold, italicize, or format text on your profile (WTF, right?), and the only way to include bullet points is to just copy and paste bullets in as characters, which means if the text wraps it doesn't indent like it would with a real bullet. You might as well just stick asterisks in there.

I reviewed around 30 influential UXer's profiles and only three of them were using bullet points in their job descriptions. It took me a little while to notice this, but once I did I couldn't unsee it. That's when I realized that skimming through a few brief conversational paragraphs was far easier than trying to scan through a hodgepodge of wrapping bullet points. I immediately changed all of my job descriptions on LinkedIn to paragraphs.

EXPERIMENT

Since these are just my own observations about LinkedIn, I recommend experimenting with your own profile and how you engage with others and see what happens. Turn it into your own little user research/usability project. You can easily measure your results with profile views, "likes," messages, referrer links to your website/portfolio, etc., and adjust accordingly.

[8]

Portfolio

Just like the poor cobbler's children and their shoes, a lot of UXers have crappy or nonexistent design portfolios.

I get it. The last thing I want to do after working on other people's UX projects all day is design my own portfolio and website. My brain is tired, plus I have to use all sorts of different skills like trying to make PowerPoint and WordPress themes bend to my will.

But a portfolio is critical. It's a requirement on almost every job posting, and recruiters that reach out to you will ask for it. And it's probably the thing that can set you apart from other job applicants the most. It's your *story*.

And when you think about it, it should be pretty straightforward, right? I mean, these were all projects you worked on so you already know all the details. And you're a UX designer. So finding a way to put it all together and make it look nice isn't rocket science.

Portfolio Format

I've researched this out the wazoo and keep hearing conflicting points of view from recruiters, hiring managers, and other UXers.

Since there are benefits to having both an online version of your portfolio and a PDF version, I believe you should have both.

ONLINE VERSION

The online version can be more high level – perhaps you focus more on your process in general, then drill down into one or two case studies. (My online portfolio doesn't even have case studies – I just use a long-page format where I talk about my process and include photos and screenshots from various projects throughout the years.)

Sometimes online job applications ask you for the link to your portfolio and provide a field for you to type it in. There's nowhere to attach a PDF. Or a recruiter or potential client is checking out your website and want a taste of what your deliverables look like and how your process works, but they're in that research stage so they're not ready to talk to you yet.

My portfolio lives on my own website (lisamurnan.com). I like it this way because I have total control over how I present the content (as long as I can figure out WordPress). I can also hook up Google Analytics and see who's viewing my portfolio. When you send recruiters and hiring managers to other websites like Behance or Dribbble to view your portfolio, you're taking them away from your home base (where they can also view *other design- ers' portfolios*) and you're totally at the mercy of that other site's user experience, which might not be as usable as something you could design yourself.

If you don't have a website and you're feeling overwhelmed by this whole portfolio thing, create the PDF version first then put it online somewhere like Dropbox so that when you're applying for jobs and they ask you for a link, you have a URL you can send them to versus an attachment.

PDF VERSION

The PDF version of your portfolio can be very detailed and contain more case studies and screenshots. It can also be customized for whoever you're sending it to and whatever job you're applying for.

Analyzing job descriptions will give you clues about how to customize your PDF portfolio. And if you've built up a collection of case studies ahead of time, you can mix and match them to quickly create a portfolio that aligns with the job description. You never know when that next opportunity will come along and what type of specific experience that company will be looking for. Does the job posting mention that financial services experience is a nice to have? Include examples of financial services work you've done. Are personas specifically mentioned? Include case studies where you created personas. Do they want somebody to design mobile experiences? Include a smartphone or tablet example.

Sometimes a PDF version of your portfolio is also going to be more convenient than the online version, like when you have a technical interview with another UXer. They're going to want to walk through several case studies in your portfolio in great detail and ask questions. You can email them (or the recruiter) the PDF version before the interview and they can print it out or zoom in on the screenshots. If it's an interview with a screen share, you can also pull up the PDF version and present it that way.

Portfolio Structure

Hiring managers and other interviewers are using your portfolio to assess your process and the reasoning behind your design decisions more than anything else. So just putting a few glossy screenshots of the finished product in there isn't going to cut it. Most projects are a team effort and it's impossible to tell from a screenshot of the finished product what part you actually had a hand in. You need to make clear what your role was and show them all the messy work that led up to that beautiful screenshot.

One great thing about UX is that you've got leeway to design a UX deliverable the way you want, based on what you think your audience needs. For example, personas all follow the same general principles, but your personas could look totally different from somebody else's personas and that's okay as long as yours are conveying what they need to (and they still look nice). The same goes for your portfolio. It's your portfolio and you're a designer, so make it unique to you. Show your personality.

I created the print version of my portfolio in PowerPoint then saved it as a PDF. I never thought I'd enjoy using PowerPoint, but I have to say that I really like how my portfolio turned out. Use whatever makes you happy, as long as it generates a nice-looking PDF that prints well.

My portfolio is structured like this:
1. Cover page
2. A little bit about myself... (1 page)
3. About this portfolio and my design process (1 page)
4. Case studies (five case studies that vary based on the job description – 10-12 pages)
5. What people say about me (testimonials) (1 page)
6. "Thank You" page with contact info

I include a lot of case studies but you don't need that many. Remember, I'm old. You need two or three good solid case studies in your portfolio. Beyond that, focus on quality, not quantity. Don't show any work that you feel is subpar or that you can't tell a good story about. Explain your process for every project (it's okay if it's different from project to project...the design process is heavily influenced by timeline, budget, type of project, etc.).

Try to show project diversity if you can. It's nice to have examples from different platforms and industries, like websites, web apps, native mobile apps, retail, financial services, etc.

Don't be afraid to include personal projects that show off your creativity and thought process. One of the case studies in my portfolio is the website I built for my husband's business (he does sporting event halftime shows with our dogs). For that project, I used tools that I don't normally use in my day job, like Word-Press and Google Analytics, and I also handled all his branding and marketing assets, like logos, business cards, banners, t-shirts, etc. I did the website singlehandedly, so all the design decisions were mine (for better or for worse!). And it's easy for me to talk about the results, because I'm tracking them first-hand every day in Google Analytics.

CASE STUDY CONTENT

Remember middle school math class and "show your work"? It's applicable here. Just like your math teacher had no way of knowing how you got to that answer if you didn't show your work, the person looking at your portfolio has no way of knowing how you got to that polished pixel-perfect screenshot in your case study unless you show how it all evolved.

You can use the handy-dandy STAR approach to structure your portfolio content.

Situation

Set the scene. Include the company name (and what they do, if it's not clear) and a project description. What was the business goal of the project? If you were redesigning something, include a "before" picture of the website/app (especially if it's horribly ugly).

Task

What was your role on the project? What were you responsible for? What deliverables were you tasked with creating? Who else did you work closely with (other UXers, business stakeholders, developers)?

Actions

What was your design process? What did you learn about your users? What design decisions did you make and why?

This is where you get into the details about what you did. Show your understanding/empathy for the user and how you reached your design solution. Include photos or screenshots of the process and talk about any tricky design challenges you came across and how you solved them.

It's okay to talk about mistakes and how you dealt with them, too. Mistakes are made on every UX project – the design process is messy.

Some things you could show:
- Screenshots (before and after)
- Site maps
- Sketches (whiteboard or paper)
- Wireframe/prototype screens
- Analytics screenshots
- Storyboards
- Journey maps
- User/task flows

I don't know why, but UX people love to show (and see) photos with Post-it Notes in them in their portfolios and on their websites. I guess Post-it Notes are sort of the unofficial UX symbol, the "UX bird."If you've worked on a project where you used

Post-it Notes, and you have a photo of them that helps you tell your story, add it to your portfolio. It'll catch the recruiter's eye, if nothing else.

Results

Show the final design, the solution you landed on. What was the outcome of the project (did it meet the business goals)? If possible, link the outcome to specific actions you took or decisions you made during the project. If your team did usability testing you can also talk about those results. What did you learn from the experience?

Plus a Little UCD

Step through the user-centered design process in your head to help you fill in any gaps. You could mention:

- Collaborating with the business to understand their goals.
- Conducting research to understand users' goals/needs.
- Sketching and designing solutions (user journey, storyboarding, task flows, wireframing, prototyping, visual design, iterating).
- Usability testing.
- Working with engineering to build out design (creating design assets or specs or style guides).
- Measuring results (metrics or other success criteria as defined at the beginning of the project).

UXers love to talk about the importance of telling stories. Your portfolio is a great place for storytelling. Bring your projects to life, like you were explaining them to someone in person and spreading the project artifacts out on a table in front of them.

NDA Work

Some of the projects I'm working on right now aren't available to show to the public. They're either product designs in progress or internal applications that'll never be accessible to the public. So I won't be putting any screenshots of them on my website where anybody could see them or happen across them in a Google search. But I'm happy to talk about my overall process on my website and show examples of the types of deliverables I produce and screenshots of work that has launched and is already out there for the world to see.

Work that isn't public yet or that's under a non-disclosure agreement (NDA) is tricky to show in a portfolio. Most employers are going to respect it when you protect the work of other employers or clients, understanding that if they were to hire you, you'd protect their work like that, too. There are some ways around it, most of them subpar, such as recreating the work with different content/branding, blurring out screenshots, or substituting all the content with Lorum Ipsum text.But looking at a wireframe that just says Header 1, Hero Image, Client 1, Client 2, Lorum Ipsum blah blah blah isn't going to tell hiring managers much about why you made the design decisions you did. It just looks like a generic template at that point.

If you signed an NDA or an intellectual property agreement before you started designing something and it's now public, it should be safe to put the screenshots in your portfolio. Anybody can see the screens now. If it's something behind a login but it's still available to the public (meaning somebody can pay for it or sign up for an account and get access to it), I'd also feel just fine putting that in my portfolio. If you still feel uncomfortable, add that case study to the PDF version of your portfolio but don't put it up online anywhere (or password-protect the PDF).

Pro Tips
If you have a website, make sure you include the URL in your portfolio (I put mine in the footer).

Don't use colored backgrounds on your PDF pages! If people want to print out your portfolio they will be irritated. I made the original cover page of my portfolio turquoise blue with white text, then later (after I had already sent it to somebody) realized how much ink that would use up.

Put page numbers on your portfolio, too. If you're walking through it with somebody you want to be able to say, "If you flip to page 7, I can walk you through the case study for Company X…"

Like a good UXer, test everything out before sending it to somebody else. Email the PDF to yourself and print it out. Email the URL to yourself and click on it. View your portfolio from your phone.

Start keeping a project scrapbook (a folder on your laptop is fine) and update it as you work on projects. Include project artifacts/deliverables, notes about major milestones/decisions, design sketches, wireframe/prototype screenshots, plus photos of whiteboard sessions, workshops, user research, usability tests, etc. It is so much easier to do this while you're still working on the project or very shortly after (within two weeks of wrapping up) versus trying to dredge up all these details months or even years later.

[9]

Cover Letter

Cover letter, *whaaat?* Didn't those go out of style in the nineties?

Believe it or not, many of today's online job applications require that you attach a cover letter (or type one into a text area on the application). There may also be times when you contact a recruiter or hiring manager directly via email about a job, which is essentially a cover letter as well.

Cover letters, albeit one more step in the tedious job hunting process, are the perfect opportunity for you to tie everything together. They are direct communication between you and the company, and a good one will bring context and personality to your resume and portfolio.

Like your resume and portfolio, your cover letter should be customized for every job you apply for. In fact, it should be the most customized thing you create. Don't just crank it out as an afterthought before you hit submit on the job application.

Your goal is to convince the hiring manager that you are interested in *their* job, not just any job you can get.

For starters, stick with the same design style as your resume and portfolio (the pretty PDF versions). Use the same fonts, colors, and spacing. You could actually use the exact same header from your resume for your cover letter. Save the cover letter as a PDF so that all of your documents are in the same easy-to-open format.

The entire letter should be no longer than one page.

There is no one-size-fits-all cover letter, and how it's received will depend on who's reading it. It's going to be very subjective. But don't let that scare you into writing a safe, boring cover letter! Aim for a conversational non-pushy tone, which will go a long way toward making your cover letter stand out from everybody else's lame-ass stole-it-from-a-template cover letter.

Here's a good format to follow:
Greeting
If at all possible, avoid starting the letter with "To Whom It May Concern" or "Dear Sir or Madam." That just sounds awful. It's like getting junk mail in your mailbox. In 1957.

LinkedIn makes it relatively easy to find a contact name to address the letter to, whether it's the hiring manager or the HR person in charge of hiring (if you're applying to a small company or startup without a big UX team, this may be the only applicable name you can find.)

If you're at a total loss, go with something like "Dear Hiring Manager" or "Dear HR Manager," or "Dear Human Resources team." You could even just say "Hello," or leave the greeting off entirely.

Top section
Write one or two paragraphs that talk about why you're interested in the position and what you admire about the company or what you have in common with it. It's okay to sound excited as long

as you're not over the top about it. It's also nice to let them know where you heard about the job posting (as long as you don't do it like in the "Lame" example below).

Try to give a specific reason for why the job is exciting to you in the first paragraph. Also, make sure you include the job title (copy it exactly from the job posting) in the first sentence, so that a recruiter or HR person who is skimming it can quickly understand the context.

Example first sentence:
Lame: "I am applying for the UX Designer position as seen on LinkedIn."

Good: "I'm interested in joining your team as a UX Designer because I've been a fan of <Your Website/App> for years and would love the opportunity to work on it." (Only if you really do use their website/app, though!)

Find ways to align your values to their mission statement.

Here's an example:
"I am impressed with your company's mission and passion – my 16-year-old son has just started researching colleges and the thought of him weighed down by student loan debt stresses me out. <Your Company> seems poised to make a big difference in a lot of people's lives."

If you've read great reviews about the company on Glassdoor or a complimentary article in the *New York Times*, let them know. It shows that you did your due diligence researching them and that you appreciate why their company would be an awesome place to work.

Middle section

Your cover letter should not just regurgitate your resume in paragraph form. The person reading your cover letter already has your resume and can refer to it if they want.

That being said, it's okay to mention your resume with something like this: "As you will see from the attached resume, I have consulted with several startups on fast-paced and innovative web and mobile projects."

Include a paragraph or two that highlights your experience, education (if relevant), and anything else that demonstrates why you'd be a great fit. Don't actually say "As you can see, I'd be a great fit" because that's presumptuous, and sounds like you copied it right off a cover letter template. Let the recruiter or hiring manager reach that conclusion for themselves.

If the job description asks for SaaS knowledge, include a sentence or two about any SaaS projects you've worked on. If the description mentions specific design activities (like user research or prototyping) or deliverables (like customer journey maps) briefly mention your experience with them. If it's relevant, talk about your experience collaborating with users or engineers or stakeholders. Bonus points if you can weave any or all of this naturally into a paragraph about your design process and/or user-centered design.

Also, try to read between the lines of the job posting to see what they really need. A startup is going to need somebody who's independent and proactive and willing to jump in and take on whatever is necessary. A large UX team is going to need somebody who plays nicely with others and is good at following an established process, presenting to stakeholders, collaborating with other UXers, etc. Show that you understand what they need.

Don't parrot the job description back at them. If the job description reads, "We are looking for someone who has a passion for creating beautiful digital interfaces from start to finish," do not say "I am passionate about creating beautiful digital interfaces from start to finish."

Bottom section

This just needs to be a paragraph summing things up and thanking them for their time and consideration.

You can also let them know you look forward to hearing from them, but don't be obnoxious about it.

Obnoxious: "I'll be looking forward to hearing from you soon." (Even worse: "I'll call you to schedule an interview.")

Better: "I appreciate your consideration and look forward to hearing from you."

Wrap up with something simple like "Best," "Sincerely," "Warmest Regards," or my personal favorite, "Best to you and the team."

[10]

Website

If you're designing for the web and calling yourself a UX designer, it does make sense to have a website. It's also nice to have a home base that you can point people to from social media and where you can showcase your portfolio. You can use Google Analytics to track visitors to your website, too.

Mine is just a simple WordPress site hosted on Bluehost – I chose a theme (Avada) that I could customize (colors, fonts, layout, etc.) because some of the WordPress themes look slick but are terrible from a usability standpoint. You don't want to represent yourself as this badass UX designer but then have a website that's hard to use or has obvious design issues. I want some *control*, man.

I don't have any experience with Squarespace or Wix or any of the other website builders so I can't comment on them, but it doesn't matter what you create your site in as long as it looks nice on the front-end. You're not applying for a coding job, so who cares if your backend code has Squarespace comments all over it?

The deals are changing all the time, but while I'm writing this Bluehost has a deal for $3.95/month web hosting plus a free domain name (and it comes with website building tools and free WordPress installations). And the Avada theme I bought was $60, so you're not looking at a huge investment here. You can use a free WordPress theme if you want, but you may not be able to customize it as much as you'd like. Make sure whatever theme you pick is responsive and looks good on your phone.

I'm lucky enough to have a unique name so I got lisamurnan.com as my domain name, but you might have to be more creative. You could include your middle name or initial along with your first/ last name, or come up with a company name or add the word "consulting" to the end of your name or something like that.

Site Layout and Design

My site is very simple and just has a home page, an "About" page, a "Work With Me" page (with sub-pages for my process and the different consulting services I offer), a "Contact" page (but contact info should also be on every page), and a section for this book and its resources.

You can include a blog if you think you'll be able to keep up with it, plus anything else that you feel would add to your site's user experience. It depends on who your target audience is and what you're trying to do.

Keep your site really clean-looking. If you're not a visual designer don't stress out – it doesn't need to have fancy logos or graphics on it. I just used a Google font for my "logo" (my name), found some cool designy-looking art on Shutterstock for my hero & background images, then scattered photos (both my own and free photos from Pixabay) throughout the other pages.

For the headers and body content, I used two Google fonts (one serif and one sans serif) that looked good together – if you search on "google font combinations" you'll get some great recommendations.

Then I modified the default colors for fonts, buttons, etc. and voila, a nice professional website.

You can disable a lot of the default WordPress theme features that make your website confusing or clunky. For example, some WordPress themes have hover states on blog post thumbnails or portfolio thumbnails with a slew of icons that don't make sense. They look pretty and they fill up the space nicely but what's supposed to happen when you click on them? If *you're* confused when you first see something in your theme, your site's visitors are going to be confused, too. Read through the theme's documentation and figure out how to turn off features like that.

[11]

Google Yourself

Have you googled yourself lately? Or ever? You might be surprised by what you find.

Several years ago, one of my coworkers was trying to find the Skype userid for another coworker so she could chat with him about a project they were both working on. Imagine her surprise when she googled his name and saw on the very first page of search results a Whistleblower 9 news report about how he owed $134,000 in back child support payments on seven different children and was wanted by the state of South Carolina. And there was no doubt it was him because his mugshot was right there in the article. *Oops.*

When you're job hunting, people will google your name. They want to see if you're really who your resume/portfolio represents you to be. Luckily, you have some control over the search results,

Feeling Lucky Today?
Ok, so let's take the plunge – go to Google and enter in your name. If you have a Google account (Gmail, Google+, etc.) and are already logged in, you will also need to switch to a public view so that you're seeing unfiltered search results (Google personalizes your search results based on your profile).

You can do this from the search results by clicking on Settings (right under the search box) then "Hide Private Results."

What do you see?
- Does somebody else with the same name as you dominate the first few pages of search results? (And do they have a mugshot?)
- Does your name only pop up in random 5k race results or a high school reunion blurb?
- Is there something negative associated with your name on a website you have no control over?
- Are crickets chirping on the search results page (along with a link to ancestry.com and public records websites)?

You can fix it.

No, you can't delete things that are on other websites. You can try contacting the person who owns the website and asking them to remove the content, but if that doesn't work you're pretty much out of luck. Google won't remove anything from their search results unless there is a valid legal reason to do so (like identity theft – view Google's Removal Policy). But here's what you *can* do – you can create positive new content that pushes down the outdated or third-party content to the second or third page of results. Not many people are going to look beyond the first page or two of search results, especially if they're just trying to get a feel for what you're all about or find you on social media.

Tips
- Make sure you reference your name the same way everywhere. When I got married a few years ago, I was referencing myself about four different ways online (maiden name, married name, maiden + married name, married name with middle initial) and it diluted my search results.

- Be consistent across all the social media profiles you create. Use the same name, email address, location, job description, etc. so that it's easy for people (and Google) to see that all your online profiles are related to the same person.
- Take advantage of cross-referencing. Most social media sites allow you to link to other social media sites from your profile.
- Think about how people will search for you and include those keywords in your profile. If you have a common name, someone searching might include your city name to narrow down the results, for example ("John Smith Atlanta"), so be sure to include that keyword in your profile description.

Buy a domain name and create your own website

Domain names are cheap – $12 or so a year (even less if you pay for multiple years at once). And your name in a domain name is one of the most powerful things you can have in terms of controlling search results. When you search for my name in Google, my website comes up as #3, right under LinkedIn and Facebook.

Some of us are lucky because our names aren't very common. I was able to buy both my maiden name and my married name with no problem. I also snapped up my husband's name and both my kids' names. You'll have to get creative if your name is already taken. If the goal is better Google results, having some form of your name in the domain name is better than a company name, but either way make sure your name is prominently featured throughout your website's content to help with search engine optimization.

Also, do yourself a favor and set your domain name to auto-renew so you never have to worry about it again.

Create a LinkedIn profile

LinkedIn is a very high authority site in Google's eyes. My LinkedIn profile is currently #1 in my list of search results.

You should have a LinkedIn profile already if you're job hunting! Fill out your profile as completely as you can, and customize your public profile URL (which means your name would appear in the link, like this: www.linkedin.com/in/yourname, versus a long line of gobbledygook after the LinkedIn part). Having your name in the URL will help its rankings.

Make sure your profile is set to be visible to the public.

Create a Twitter profile

Create a profile, add a photo, and link to your website. It's okay if you don't tweet. I'm hardly ever on Twitter and it still shows up on the first page of my search results.

Create a YouTube channel and post a video

YouTube ranks really high in Google search results (not a big surprise since Google owns YouTube). And YouTube's own search engine is the second largest behind Google, so it's worth it to get some video content on there if you have something to share.

YouTube is currently #9 on my list of search results. Like LinkedIn, you can also claim your own custom URL to match your name.

Other Observations

Pinterest and Instagram photos show up high in the search results if your name is part of the photo's title or description.

My WordPress sites, even the half-baked ones or ones with passwords, show up all over page two of my search results since my name is listed as an admin or an author on the site.

Even though nobody uses Google+, if you have a Google+ profile it will rank high in the search results.

All of this is handy info if your goal is to populate the top page or two of Google search results with positive and current information about yourself and push other stuff down.

Follow Through

Your search results can vary wildly while you're busy making changes to your social media profiles and working on your own website. It's fun to see your efforts pay off and it doesn't take Google long to find the new content and rank it.

A few other tips:

- Create an alert on your name. You can easily do this at Google Alerts. That way if your name pops up on a website anywhere, you'll be notified via email. You can also create searches on your email address, phone number, etc.
- Keep your social media profiles updated across the board if you move, switch jobs, etc.

[12]

Preparing for the Interview

My friend Mandy Linton, who is the UX Director at a major insurance company, shared with me her process when she's filling a role. "I read the resume, do a Google search on their name, then go to LinkedIn and finally Pinterest. I do this with everyone I interview," she says. "*Everyone.* If they pass that screening process, then it's a phone interview with me, then with one or two of my senior folks, then if they pass all that, they come in for a face to face visit with the team."

Screening Interview

Rock-n-roll! Your resume and portfolio caught the attention of the right people (and your Google results and Pinterest boards didn't scare anybody) and now they want to do an initial screening interview. This is typically done by a recruiter or someone in the HR department and only lasts 30 minutes or so. They probably aren't going to ask you difficult user experience questions, they just want to determine whether or not you'll be a good fit, when you'd be available to start, what your salary requirements are, etc. They may ask for some clarification around the skills you listed on your resume. They'll also tell you more about the company and the role.

How to prepare for this interview and any follow-up interviews

- *Research the company like crazy.* Look at the company website (duh), Twitter feed, LinkedIn and Facebook pages, YouTube videos of product demos, Glassdoor reviews, and anything else that comes up in a Google search. Read the company blog to find out about new products or features they're rolling out. Read client case studies to understand clients' needs and business goals. Figure out who their competitors are. Research is one of the most critical things you can do to prepare. You need to walk into that interview and show them that you know what their company is all about and that you're interested in what they are doing.

- *Find the company's mission statement.* It may be on the careers section of their website. Some companies, like Amazon, take their internal values so seriously that the way you answer value-related questions may count more than anything else.

- *If you know the names of the people you'll be interviewing with, look them up.* Check LinkedIn (use the Private Mode feature so they don't know you're stalking them), Facebook, Medium, Twitter, anywhere you think they may have a presence (obviously Google will help you with this part). If you find something or someone (like a hobby or a mutual friend or former coworker) in common with them and it comes up naturally in conversation, great. If it'll come across as too creepy/contrived, don't mention it but use that info to help you understand their personality and motivations a little better.

- *Go back through the job posting and take it apart line by line.* What might they ask you about? What specific skills are they looking for? Do they mention any tools by name (like Sketch or Axure)? You can anticipate a lot of what they'll ask you by deconstructing the job posting.

- *If it's a phone interview, make sure your sound is good.* If you're using your cell phone, plan to talk in a quiet room where your connection doesn't blip in and out. Make sure your phone is charged. Use good headphones. Have your finger ready to hit the mute button. Put all the barky dogs away. I have 11 dogs so this is an issue for me.

- *If it's a video interview, set up and test the area ahead of time.* I like to sit at a desk in my bedroom with a clean dresser and plain wall behind me (I'll put a plant on the dresser for a little pizzazz). Make sure your microphone sounds okay and you look good on camera and there's nothing distracting around you. I always recruit my daughter to help with this. She'll test with me on Skype and Google Hangouts, and we'll reverse places so I can see what she looks like sitting in front of my computer in my room.

- *If you're going to be sharing your screen, sanitize it ahead of time.* Close everything on your computer other than your email, browser, resume, and portfolio. Hide your browser's bookmark bar. Empty your cache. Disable notifications.

- *Have a copy of your attractive resume and PDF portfolio pulled up.* Make sure they contain the same content as the ones you sent when you applied, assuming you customized them for this job.

- *Create a cheat sheet with different questions and answers on it.* If it's a phone interview you can have it right on the desk in front of you. If it's a video interview you can tape the most common questions & answers up in front of you on a wall or chair or something. It can just be index cards or Post-it Notes with bullet points to help prompt you. (Sample interview questions and design exercises will be covered extensively in the next chapter).

- **_Remember, they think you're qualified._** Otherwise they wouldn't be interviewing you. Whenever you get nervous, remind yourself of this.

Technical Interview

If the screening interview goes well, the next step is usually a technical interview with a UXer (perhaps even the hiring manager) who will quiz you on your UX knowledge and walk through your portfolio with you. This will probably be on the phone or video with a screen share.

You will be asked specific questions about your process and what tools you like to use. You can also ask them questions about the team, the project you'd be working on, how everybody works together, etc.

Behavioral Interview

After the technical interview may be a behavioral interview with someone else in the company to see if you're a culture fit. This is when they'll ask those "Tell me about a time when…" questions.

Have a list of examples from your past ready to go and use the STAR approach to help you structure replies to each question.

Make sure you study the company's mission statement and anything about their culture you can get your hands on. If one of their values is "entrepreneurial spirit," find ways to talk about your own entrepreneurial spirit. (However, if you have no entrepreneurial spirit, please don't pretend you do. You want to be yourself as much as you can so that you don't end up getting the job but hating it.)

... And Beyond

If you make it through all of these interviews, you're doing great. At this point, they'll probably have you talk to other members of the team, both UXers and stakeholders like a product owner or a business analyst or an engineer, and of course you'll talk with the hiring manager.

In my experience, it takes at least three phone/video interviews (including the initial screening) before they're willing to bring you in for an in-person interview. In-person interviews cost them a lot of money and employee time. For my current job, I did all my interviewing over the phone or video, and was hired sight-unseen (except for two video interviews). The first time I stepped foot into the office was for orientation. This is happening much more often these days.

In-Person Interviews

If you're invited to an in-person interview, be prepared for either back-to-back interviews all day long and/or a panel interview where you sit in a conference room with a lot of other people and present your portfolio and/or work on a design exercise. The company should pay for all of your expenses, including airfare, transportation, hotel, and food. Some companies have you pay out of pocket and then reimburse you after you fill out an expense report.

Bring your laptop or tablet (fully charged) with your portfolio on it. Bring two printouts of your portfolio, too, just in case. Print out several copies of your resume as well.

In 2012, I interviewed in person at a company in San Diego. They gave me a design exercise to work on five days prior to the interview. Here's what the schedule looked like on interview day:

9:00 – 10:00am
Hiring Manager & Team: "Job Talk"
This was 13 UX people and me in a conference room. They grilled me on my experience and then had me present the results of the design exercise they gave me (essentially a heuristic review of their existing checkout process and wireframes to show how I'd improve it).

10:00 – 11:00am
‹Name›, User Interaction Designer
‹Name›, Senior User Interaction Designer

11:00 – 12:00pm
‹Name›, Lead User Interaction Designer
‹Name›, Senior User Interaction Designer

12:00 – 1:00pm
‹Name›, Lead User Researcher
‹Name›, Associate Manager, Software Design Engineering

1:00 – 2:00pm
‹Name›, Lead User Interaction Designer
‹Name›, User Interaction Designer

2:00 – 3:00pm
‹Name›, Sr. Director, Software Development
‹Name›, Director, Product Management

Brutal. But's it just for one day, and if you practice answering all the common interview questions and walking through a couple of case studies from your portfolio ahead of time you'll be ready for most of what they throw at you. The one question that fazed me during this interview was when one of the Senior Interaction Designers asked if I might be too conservative for their company (my last few jobs were in financial services and I was dressed in a skirt and blazer for the interview, while the rest of them were in jeans and t-shirts). Anybody who knows me would have laughed out loud at that "too conservative" comment. I guess I should have worn something that showed off my tattoos, and maybe dropped an F-bomb or two.

But that just goes to show that I should have done better research into their culture. If I had, I would have probably found some photos of their happy employees at work, wearing their jeans and t-shirts. Then I would have worn nice jeans with the blazer instead of the skirt.

I got the job anyway.

"Practice" Interviews

Consider interviewing for positions you're not that interested in. You won't be as nervous because you won't care as much, and you can get first-hand experience answering questions like "So, tell me about yourself" and seeing what else they come up with.

Plus, each company has a different interview process. Some do all phone interviews, others use Skype, others use Google Hangouts, others use more obscure video conferencing software (like appear.in). The more experience you can get with this stuff, the better. You'll get good at sharing documents, finding the mute button quickly, and figuring out which camera angle makes you look the awesomest.

The Charm Factor

It really does help to be charming. I'm not sure how you can achieve this if you're not a naturally charming person but do your best. If you're likable, the person interviewing you is going to be able to picture how you'll be in a room with clients or stakeholders and how you'll come across during design critiques, workshops, executive presentations, and user interviews. People hire people they like.

When you first meet somebody, greet them by their name ("Hi Michael, it's great to meet you") and a smile and make small talk for a minute while you're getting settled. If you can make them laugh, even better.

But follow their lead! If they're being professional, you be professional. If they're being outgoing, you be outgoing. If you're sitting across from a dry serious senior UX designer who is asking you about your UX experience, don't launch into a bubbly "I just *love* UX, I am *soooo* passionate about it!" spiel or you're going to annoy the hell out of them.

Test and Iterate

If you don't make it all the way through the interview process, don't despair. Learn whatever you can from the experience and iterate from there.

Treat each interview like a usability test of sorts.

You may not be able to get direct feedback from your interviewers (although if you're feeling brave you can ask them), but through observation you should be able to tell what you struggled with or what didn't sync up between what they were looking for and what you had to offer.

Sometimes this isn't your fault and there's nothing you could have done about it. Maybe they hired internally. Maybe they wanted someone with SaaS experience and you've never worked on a SaaS project. It doesn't mean you're not a good designer.

Let this quote about interviewing from senior product designer Weston Karnes's Medium article "Learnings from Product Design Interviews" cheer you up:

"Don't take it personal. Let's face it, interviews are dumb. People are asked to make assumptions and conclusions off entirely incomplete information. The sooner you realize this, the better."

[13]

Interview Questions and Design Exercises

Preparation is Key

Below are a lot of potential questions you may be asked during an interview. As you read through them you may think, "I have no idea how I'd answer this!" That's why you need to do the work up front. You don't want to be fumbling for an answer during the interview. Hoping that they won't ask a certain question isn't a good strategy.

Take time now to go back through past jobs and projects and find examples you can use to answer these questions. Read through your portfolio and resume and try to jog your memory. I did this recently and seriously couldn't remember anything past two jobs ago. I had to go through old emails and deliverables to find examples (and there were some doozies...no wonder I blocked it all out!).

Create cheat sheets to have nearby during an interview (if it's a phone or video interview, you can keep them in front of you. If it's an in-person interview you can read through them in the car right beforehand). When you have it all thought through and written down ahead of time and you get a question like, "Tell me about a time when you struggled on a project and how you handled it," it's almost like you're taking a test at school and you have the answer written right there on your arm. It feels like cheating. But it's not!

Types of Interview Questions

Interview questions are going to vary depending on the UX maturity of the company. (Jakob Nielsen has a great set of articles about the eight stages of UX maturity, just google "Corporate UX Maturity" to find them.)

If UX is new to the company, expect to get asked questions about how you'll fit into the existing process/methodology (like Agile), how you'll evangelize UX across the company, and how you'll work with engineers/product owners. I was the second UX hire at the company I work for now, so there was only one UX person on staff to ask me the skill-based questions. The rest of the people I interviewed with were engineers, business analysts, data architects, and technology managers.

They didn't ask me to walk through my portfolio and they didn't care what tools I used, as long as I could easily share my design ideas with them. I was asked by several different interviewers how I would deal with developers who had strong opinions of their own about designs and how I would convince them to go with my design recommendations. (It was pretty clear what I'd be doing if I got hired!) The interviews were all one-on-one and for the most part conversational.

In contrast, when UX is firmly established inside an organization expect to get asked very detailed questions about the user-centered design process, tools, and deliverables. Expect to walk through your portfolio in great detail, and be questioned about why you made some of the design decisions that you did. You'll probably be asked to participate in a design exercise. Interviews will be more formal and contain pre-determined skills-related or behavioral questions.

Sample Interview Questions

Some of the sample questions below were copied directly from Glassdoor's "Interviews" section, while others were what I had written down from previous interviews or interview prep.

The "right" answer will often vary depending on what company you're interviewing with (keeping in mind their mission/culture and the type of work they do), the person you're interviewing with, and the specific role you're interviewing for.

For UX roles, remember that they're trying to understand your process and whether or not you understand the user-centered design process and the value of user research and usability testing. They also want to know if you're going to be able to take design feedback well and if you're going to be able to interact professionally with stakeholders. When in doubt, build your answers around your (user-centered design inspired) process and collaboration skills.

Write down your answers to the top questions and practice saying them out loud over and over until it feels smooth. (If you're not a memorizer, or are afraid you'll sound too scripted, riff off bullet points instead.)

TELL ME ABOUT YOURSELF

You are going to hear this question so many times that you might as well write your elevator speech ahead of time and practice it in the mirror until it feels natural.

It is usually the first question an interviewer will ask. This is an awkward open-ended question and if you don't have a good answer prepared you can end up rambling for a few minutes and then feeling like you got off on the wrong foot for the interview.

Instead of "Tell me about yourself," think of it as "Give me a brief professional overview of yourself." Craft a one-to-two-minute answer that sums up your career (especially your current job/projects) and your UX skills and design process. You could include a story about how you got interested/involved in UX to begin with.

Do not take the interviewer through a chronological list of all your jobs since high school, or offer up a lot of personal details. Focus on what's most relevant for this particular job.

Go back through the job posting and look at it from the hiring manager's perspective – what kind of person do they really want to hire? What skills do they call out specifically? Weave these attributes into your answer.

WALK ME THROUGH SOMETHING FROM YOUR PORTFOLIO

If you've structured your case studies well (using STAR or a similar method), you'll make it easy on yourself when this question pops up.

Choose a case study that either best matches the job description (if the hiring manager is looking for someone to design a mobile app, walk them through a mobile app you worked on) or that showcases your design process from end-to-end. (Either way, they are going to be *very* interested in your process.)

Use the case study in your portfolio as a guide, but improvise a bit while you're talking about it – don't just read it verbatim off the page. Add a little color by throwing in details about how you worked with business stakeholders, or insights you gained from user research that weren't included in the original case study. Tell the story behind the photos and screenshots in the case study – those can be hard for reviewers to make sense of on their own, since they're often cropped or reduced in size to fit inside the portfolio.

Some places, like Google, will question you on your design choices (maybe even tiny things, like why your drop-down menu looks the way it does) so familiarize yourself with every screenshot in your portfolio and be prepared to explain your design rationale.

WHAT IS YOUR DESIGN PROCESS?

Remember, there is no one perfect process – it's going to vary based on the type of project, technical constraints, goals, timeline, budget, etc. So don't stress about your process not being "right." Weave user-centered design principles into your explanation – no matter what the process is, it's always important for UX designers to ask the right questions and to do everything they can to understand and involve their users.

Related questions:
- What's your process for working with other designers, developers, or product managers?
- Let's say I have a new project for you to work on – what's the first thing you'd ask me about it?

EVALUATE A WEBSITE OR APP

The interviewer may ask you to critique their existing product and offer suggestions for how you'd improve it (this was the type of design exercise I was given in San Diego). You may feel like you're giving them hours of free consulting advice, but it's a great way for them to assess whether you understand their business model or product, and how you will fit into the team. And get free consulting advice at the same time.

Facebook asks interviewees to evaluate their favorite website or app and to analyze why they think the designer made the decisions they made, then asks if they agree with those decisions.

Related questions:
- What's one of your favorite apps/websites and one of your least favorite, and why?
- How would you improve our UX experience? (Wayfair)
- What app/tool/thing do you use often that you would redesign if you could? (Google)
- Describe a company that has great UX and why.
- What company/app/website do you admire when it comes to UX?
- Looking at this product, what UX issues do you notice?

BEHAVIORAL QUESTIONS

Questions like these are meant to reveal how you deal with failure or challenges. Everybody has them in their career. Interviewers want to see that you are humble and that you learn from your mistakes and grow professionally as a result.

Examples:
- Tell me about a time when you went against the whole team because you believed your solution was correct. (Amazon)
- Describe for me a project that went badly wrong. Why did it go wrong, and what did you personally learn from it?
- Describe a situation where you used your influence and persuasion to successfully convince someone to see things your way. (Amazon)
- Give me an example of a project you were proud of. Why were you proud of it and what obstacles did you have to overcome? (Amazon)

- Tell me about a time when you had to advocate for a controversial design decision. What did you do? How was that received? What did you do when people disagreed with you? Would you approach it the same way if you had to do it again?
- Tell me about one of your projects where you felt you made an impact.
- Explain a time that you had to persuade a stakeholder or engineer to approve a particular design idea.
- How do you deal with people who have a strong opinion about how a certain feature should be designed, but you disagree that it's a good user experience?
- There are times when a team member will not agree with your decision or plan. Tell me about a time when you encountered this on a project, and how you dealt with it. What was the outcome?
- How would you handle someone that is difficult to work with? (Amazon)
- Tell me about a time where you had to become a product expert. (Amazon)
- How do you resolve different opinions or solutions within your team or with the client? (Amazon)
- Tell us about a time you made a mistake in a professional setting. How did you fix the mistake and what did you learn from it? (Home Depot)

YOUR CAREER GOALS AND WORK STYLE
Examples:
- Why do you want to work here?
- Why do you want to leave your current company? (PayPal)
- Describe the work environment you are most successful in and why. (Home Depot)
- What do you need to improve upon? (Home Depot)
- What can you bring to the table that will affect the team positively?

UX-SPECIFIC QUESTIONS
Examples:
- What is User Experience?
- How do you know your design is good?
- How do you know when a design is done? (Costco)
- How do you define UX design (or UX designer)?
- What was a challenging design problem you had to solve and how did you solve it?
- How do you feel about native mobile versus mobile web in terms of the user experience?
- Think of a long-term project in your portfolio. If you had two more months to work on it, what would you have done differently? What would have you added or continued to refine?
- Where do you get inspiration from? Who in the industry do you follow and read?
- What research methods do you use? (Facebook)
- How would you give feedback on a design that you thought was bad?
- How would you communicate your findings to different stakeholders?
- Describe a project where you've dealt with a very complex design problem. (Lucid Software)
- How have you thought about designing for accessibility? (Google)
- How did you get into User Experience? (Home Depot)
- In a form, what do you prefer for the field titles, aligned to the right or to the left? and why? (RSA Security)
- What has been your experience with agile/iterative software development?
- Can you tell me more about your previous experience at ____ and what methodologies you used? (Google)
- Will you please give me an example of how you used metrics to inform your design process? (Wells Fargo)

- How do you handle a situation where you were expected to design an interface with very little, or ambiguous software requirements? (Navitaire)

WHAT IS YOUR GREATEST WEAKNESS

Please don't answer this question with "I'm a perfectionist" or "I'm a workaholic" (or even worse, "I can't think of any"). Everybody knows this is bullshit. Your interviewer isn't going to be thinking to themselves, "Oh wow, really? It will be awesome to get a workaholic on the team!"

This question is about seeing how self-aware you are and how willing you are to improve/learn/grow. Talk about a self-identified gap in your skills and how you're working to improve it.

This is a little tricky, because you don't want to say something that would make you sound unqualified for the job ("Well, I'm really not a very good designer yet, but I'm working on it!") or like an intolerant asshole ("I can't stand it when I have to sit near somebody who chews loudly").

Try to come up with something that is related to the job but not a critical job skill. You could talk about how you're working on your presentation skills by volunteering to present in your local Meetup group, or how you have a tendency to be disorganized so you've created a system (calendar, Evernote to-do list, etc.) that is working great. It's all about presenting the weakness *and* the solution.

CURVEBALL / WEIRD QUESTIONS

Google used to be notorious for its curveball interview questions but stopped when its data showed that they were ineffective. Laszlo Bock told the *New York Times*, "We found that brainteasers are a complete waste of time. How many golf balls can you fit into an airplane? How many gas stations in Manhattan? A complete waste of time. They don't predict anything. They serve primarily to make the interviewer feel smart."

In 1999, during the dot-com boom, I interviewed with an "e-business consultancy" in NYC and got my first taste of the intentionally stressful interview. The interviewer, a distracted VP, walked into the room where I had been sitting for a while, sat behind the desk facing me and asked, "So. Why should we hire you?" Then he put his feet up on the desk and drank his Dr. Pepper. I can't even remember how I answered the question, I can only remember that hot flush of embarrassment and anxiety and pissed-off-ness as he sat there all cool and smug, waiting for me to respond. I got the job, but I'm not sure if it's because I passed this particular test.

There's no way of telling what somebody will ask you. Just be prepared for anything in advance and don't take it personally. It's all just a big game.

Design exercises

Here are some real design exercises that were recently given to user experience job candidates during interviews (pulled directly from Glassdoor's "Interviews" section).

- Design an elevator panel for a building with 1,000 floors. (Cornerstone OnDemand, Nov 2017)
- Design a dashboard for analytic data. (MemberSuite, Nov 2017)
- Design a mobile checkout process. (Virtusa, Sep 2017)
- Redesign a Nike shoe page. (Red Ventures, Aug 2017)
- Design an automated subway ticket dispenser. The machine has only three buttons (with programmable LCD screens next to each so you can change its label) and a changeable, scrolling display at the top. (Lifion, July 2017)

- There is a new residential skyscraper that also has a restaurant on top. Access to all apartments and the restaurant are secured behind a locked door. Design an interface that will be on the first floor and take the place of a door person. (Google, April 2017)
- Design an alarm clock with only three buttons. (Google)
- Redesign a nutritional label. (Isobar, Oct 2017)
- Pick a specific portion of a ride scheduling app – i.e. scheduling a ride on a van – and whiteboard out the process for scheduling the ride and confirming your check in on the bus. (Ridecell, Sept 2017)
- Design a scheduling system for employees to adjust and view their shifts. (Processing Point, Aug 2017)
- Prepare and conduct a mock user interview. (Cox Automotive, July 2017)
- Design an app for a pizza delivery service. (Salesforce, May 2017)
- Design a 1,000-story building so that people can efficiently get out of the building during rush hours (lunch hours). (LinkedIn, April 2017)
- Solve for a person trying to find a location within a campus with multiple buildings like Google. The interface must be a kiosk designed as a digital receptionist. (EMS Software, April 2017)
- How would you design an elevator for a 1,000-floor building? (Amazon, Oct 2016)

Most of these design exercises are 45-60 minutes long and are done on a whiteboard or paper. You'll notice that the 1,000-floor building question comes up a lot (I'm assuming they're talking about the elevator interface, not actually designing where it would be in the building). Don't panic. It's supposed to be a hard question. You're not being judged on whether you come up with the right answer or not, they're watching to see how you think, how you approach the problem, how you collaborate with the other team members, and how you take feedback.

The best way to handle an exercise like this is to ask a lot of questions. Validate your assumptions. What is the elevator going to be used for? Is it only for people or will it be transporting something else? What are the business goals for this elevator? Do they plan to split the elevators up into banks of 100 floors or just have every elevator handle all 1,000 floors? Are there peak times you need to consider? Focus on user goals, too. What are the users' needs and pain points? Maybe you even create some quick ad-hoc personas on one corner of the whiteboard.

You can also talk about how you'd go about researching elevator interfaces if you were actually working on the project. You're probably not going to have a chance to google stuff during your whiteboard exercise, but if this was a real project we'd all be out researching really tall buildings and different elevator setups. We might even go downtown and ride a bunch of different elevators to experience it firsthand.

Once you narrow things down to a solid set of assumptions and user goals you can start sketching. You could start with the user journey (versus actual screen interfaces), which could just be a linear set of boxes and arrows on the whiteboard describing every step of the user's interaction with the elevator. Then you could add notes and questions under each step.

For example: User enters building and walks to elevator.

Questions: What would the user expect to see? Up/Down buttons they can push? A security scanner they could run their phone or an ID card over to validate they lived/worked in the building? An indication of where the elevator is currently and/or how long it will take to reach them? Read Don Norman's *The Design of Everyday Things,* it will help you understand how to design everything from doors to washing machines to web apps.

YOUR TURN TO ASK THE QUESTIONS

Remember this is a two-way street. You're interviewing them as much as they're interviewing you. Listen to their stories and how they deliver design feedback. Are these the kind of people you'd enjoy working with?

Here are few ideas to get you started, but really, it's going to depend on who you're interviewing with and what the specific job is. Just make sure that you get all your questions answered, because otherwise it's going to be like that reality show *Married at First Sight.*

- Can you describe a typical day or week in the position?
- What kind of access to end users would I have?
- How does UX fit into the Agile process here?
- What project or task would you want me to dive in and work on immediately?
- What's the most challenging thing about your job (or the department or the company) right now?
- How would you describe the culture here?
- What differentiates good UX designers from ones who are really great, in your opinion?
- Tell me about the stakeholders (business, dev team, etc.) I'd be working with. How/how often would I be interacting with them?
- How is performance evaluated and rewarded here?
- What do people love about working here?
- What types of people are successful here and what types are not?
- When do you expect to make a hiring decision?

Thank-You Notes

Don't worry, I'm not going to tell you to get custom note cards printed up and send hand-written thank-you notes to everybody you just interviewed with. Just send them an email. (Besides, by the time your snail-mail card got there, the position might already be filled.)

Yes, sending a thank-you note matters. Not only is it the polite thing to do, but it shows that you're still interested in the job after the interview.

You don't have to write anything elaborate. Just thank them for the opportunity and their time. If you and the interviewer talked about something during the interview that's worth referencing, go ahead and mention that, too.

If possible, thank each person you interviewed with (individually! No group emails!) within 24 hours of the interview. It should be pretty easy to figure out what somebody's email address is – you may already have it in an email invite from your interview, or it's obvious that the whole company uses a first initial + last name @ companyname.com format, or if all else fails you can ask the recruiter for it. You could also message them on LinkedIn (especially if it's a recruiter who originally contacted you that way).

[14]

Money

Salaries

How much can you expect to make?

Below are some UX designer salaries pulled from Justin Baker's Medium article "2018's UX Designer Salary Forecast." Baker's numbers combine 2018 forecasts with 2017 Glassdoor and Robert Half data.

The higher numbers tend to be in cities like San Francisco (Silicon Valley) and New York, whose salaries often run one-and-a-half to two times higher than other regions.

UX DESIGNER SALARIES (ESTIMATES)
Junior UX Designer: 0-2 years of experience *$45K—88K projected starting salary in 2018* Salaries at the top of the range generally go to designers who have done internships for a year or two and have a "comprehensive" portfolio.
Mid-Level UX Designer: 2-5 years of experience *$71K—108K projected starting salary in 2018* The most common positions available. These designers have real-world experience but they're more affordable than senior designers.

UX DESIGNER SALARIES (ESTIMATES)

Senior UX Designer: 6-10 years of experience
$84K—160K projected starting salary in 2018
Baker says one of the biggest trends for 2018 will be an abundance of senior level job openings, as companies want designers who can jump right in and make an immediate impact.

Principal UX Designer: 10+ years of experience
$109K—190K projected starting salary in 2018
The old timers, like me. This is the highest level for an individual contributor. Principal designers are expected to contribute significantly to their product's (and company's) UX strategy.

A few additional takeaways from the article that were really interesting:

1. *The design industry is projected to expand by 10% or more over the next five years.* This is great news for us. Companies are finally recognizing that UX is important and that their customers expect to have good user experiences with their products.

2. *65% of UX designers are self-taught.* In a 2017 UXPin survey, 2,675 UX designers were asked "What types of design or UX programs have you completed?" 65.38% of them reported that they were self-taught. See? No fancy degrees or credentials required. You just need to jump in and start doing the work.

3. *Junior UX designer jobs will be in less demand, according to Baker.* He says that companies are looking for more experienced designers who can hit the ground running, and that as a result many junior designers will end up becoming

freelancers. As you read this, please don't despair. That, my friends, is why you're reading this book. There are junior level positions out there, and you're going to be the most qualified and prepared to get them.

Something else worth noting is that UX designer salaries tend to increase very quickly with experience. Jakob Nielsen says that UX designers can expect an increase of $5,700 per year of experience for the first five years of their career, then around $3,000 a year after that (figures are for 2017), so if you're starting out in the $50k range, that number could look closer to $65-70k after just three years in the industry.

Consulting Rates

A former student recently emailed me to ask how much she should charge for some UI/UX consulting work and my reply was sort of like riding on a UX rollercoaster, because so much of it depends on the situation.

Here's my reply verbatim:

I quote $100 hour for any type of UI/UX design work (too much trouble to differentiate it based on skill because I'm usually moving back and forth between different skills as I get something done). If they balk at that amount, I will work with them on it if it looks like it's going to be a nice bit of work (like ongoing consulting vs one 5-hour project).

But some people don't bat an eye when I quote $100/hr, so I always start out with that. :) I'm also REALLY generous when I bill them for those hours — I might put in twice as many hours as I bill them for, simply because I want to do research that they're not paying me for, or I want to work through a few different iterations of a design before showing it to them.

That way when I do bill them they feel like they got excellent work for a fair price. (So technically, I guess I really charge $50/hr, haha).

I did a lot of work for one client (he would contact me every few months for a couple of years) and after a year I lowered his rate to $75/hr because I was so familiar with what he needed me to do and it was fairly easy for me.

For your situation, getting the experience would be really awesome because it could be something you add to your resume/portfolio/interview discussions, so I wouldn't scare him off with too high a bid. Maybe somewhere between $60-75 an hour? If you had a good handle on what he wanted and could estimate reasonably well how many hours that would take you ahead of time, you could also quote him a flat rate (let's say you think it might take 10-15 hours... you could quote him $500-700). Sometimes people get scared when you quote them an hourly rate because the hours can rack up really fast and their end cost is unpredictable. Each client is a little different.

Note that the recommendation above was for some independent consulting work on a small project.

If you're getting hired through an agency to work as a full-time contractor at a company, the hourly rate will go down because you're getting paid for lots of guaranteed hours on a regular basis. Even if you're making $50 an hour, that's really good money ($2k a week, over $100k a year, if you're working 40 hours).

I mentioned it earlier and I'll bring it up again because it's worth repeating – if you need more experience and projects for your portfolio, don't get hung up on how much you're getting paid. The experience itself is the payment.

[15]

If You're at a Standstill

Do you feel like you're doing everything right but still struggling to land a job? Is it taking longer than you expected? Are the rejection letters getting you down?

Sometimes these things do just take time. You're up against a lot of other applicants for the same jobs. It's possible that you've been very close to being selected and are right on the brink of a breakthrough. Sometimes it really is just a matter of being patient and sticking with it.

Other times you may need to tweak things.

Try looking at all of this as a big experiment. A real-world usability test, where your "products" (resume, portfolio, etc.) are the things being tested. For some reason they are not converting, and we need to figure out why.

Let's run through what some of the problems might be.

NO INTERVIEWS

If you're not getting any responses to your applications, or getting form rejection emails, then it probably has something to do with your resume, cover letter, and/or portfolio. Something about them isn't compelling enough for you to get invited for an interview.

- Make sure your resume is focusing on *accomplishments* and doesn't just sound like a laundry list of job responsibilities.
- Make sure your cover letter is not just your resume in paragraph format. Do your research on the company and make a *connection* between yourself and the company.
- Find ways to bridge the gaps between your experience and what the hiring manager is asking for in the job posting. Just because you weren't called a UX designer in a past role doesn't mean you don't know how to do user research, for example – maybe you did a lot of user research as a product manager. But it's up to you to call this out. The recruiter or hiring manager isn't going to take the time to try to connect the dots between your resume and the job description.
- Make sure your portfolio is telling a good story about each project you worked on. Your case studies should include a lot of clues into your thought process and how your design evolved.
- Your portfolio should be easy to access and read. You're not making people click on little thumbnails to see some clunky slideshow modal, are you? Think *easy*. Think Craigslist vs iTunes. iTunes looks pretty, but it's horrible to use.
- Get a friend or hire somebody to review all your documents and proofread them for spelling and grammar. Get a UXer (preferably one at a senior level) to read through everything to see if any red flags pop up (wrong use of terminology etc.)

At this point, don't be afraid to change things up. What have you got to lose? You could conduct your very own A/B testing using your own documents. Create two different versions of your resume – different looks, different tone, different wording.

Send version A to one company and version B to another company (don't send both versions to the same company!) and see which one gets a better response. Same with your portfolio – redo it.

Create a different template. Try writing the stories in a different way. Try including different visuals. It may just be that you need more experience. You can have the nicest documentation in the world, but if you're up against somebody with equally nice documentation and more experience than you, hiring managers are usually going to pick the person with more experience.

Don't let this get you down, though, just get your ass out there and get more experience. Experience isn't some special talent that only certain people have – it's just about doing the work. Seek out freelance, find a nonprofit with a horrible website and volunteer to redesign it, create a website or app that solves a problem that you've identified, find a Hackathon project to get involved with.

Take action, baby!

INTERVIEWS BUT NO OFFERS

Are you getting interviews but not getting offers? Then it probably has something to do with how you're answering interview questions, approaching the design exercises, or your interviewing skills in general.

- Write down every interview question you've ever gotten and your ideal answer to it. Practice answering each question over and over and over until it feels natural.
- Google "UX design exercises" and figure out how other people have successfully tackled them – there are tons of articles out on Medium, Quora, etc. that talk specifically about design exercises used in interviews. Practice whiteboarding some of the example design exercises mentioned in this book or in the articles you find.
- Are you immediately jumping to designing screens during the design exercise? This isn't what interviewers want to see. They want to see your design process in action, which should include a lot of up-front question asking and thinking around

who you're designing for and what will make your design successful.

The needs-more-experience monster may be rearing its ugly head here again, too. It may be that you've nailed the application documentation (resume, portfolio, etc.), but when they bring you in for an interview it's clear that you can talk the talk but not really walk the walk. Get more experience! Practice designing real things. Get feedback. Repeat.

[16]

Parting Thoughts

If you're ever feeling like a UX poser, remember these three things:

1. ***There's more than one way to design a user experience.*** This is not like math or spelling where's there's only one right answer. If you gave 10 UX designers the exact same project to work on, they'd probably come up with 10 different design solutions.

2. ***As a UX designer, get used to being wrong.*** Even the best designs have usability issues, especially in their early stages. I can't tell you how many times I've sat behind a two-way mirror during a usability test and watched test participants struggling with something I've designed. It's humbling, that's for sure. But that's why we test, so we can identify issues and fix them in the next iteration. As designers, we're often too close to our work to see what's wrong with it, and we also forget that we know more about our website/app than our users do. What's obvious to us is not necessarily obvious to them.

3. ***Your users will save you if you let them.*** If you're following a user-centered design process and involving your users every step of the way, they will gladly point out what works and doesn't work, and give you input on how to fix whatever's broken. All you have to do is listen.

129

I love this quote from Joel Marsh, author of *UX for Beginners: A Crash Course in 100 Short Lessons*:

> *In UX, we can test things. We can design more than one solution to the same problem and see which one is better. And we can ask users which solution they prefer.*
>
> *This means UX is a special kind of design: it can be wrong. And we can prove that it's wrong.*

[17]

Conclusion

At the end of each of my UI/UX Design Certificate Programs, when it comes time to present certificates, I've developed a silly ritual. I face each student in turn, grasp their certificate in both hands, bow my head to them, and say, "Namaste, Unicorn" as I hand them their certificate.

What I'm really trying to say to them (and to you) is this:

The UX designer in me honors the UX designer in you.

I hope this book has helped you in some way on your UX career journey.

Feel free to email me at *lisamurnan@gmail.com* with your questions or stories. I would love to hear how this book has come in handy, and/or anywhere I've gotten things wrong or left important things out. You guys are my ultimate usability test.

Also, if you enjoyed the book, it would mean so much to me if you left a review on Amazon.

I've put a bunch of things on my website to help you out, including templates for resumes, cover letters, and portfolios, worksheets, and a continually-updated list of UX books, articles, tools, etc. You can find it all at *lisamurnan.com/resources*

Best of luck, my friends!

Acknowledgments

It's funny how much writing a book is like working on a UX project.

This one started out with a problem to be solved (my students kept asking me how to get a job in the industry and there was no book or comprehensive resource to point them to), moved quickly into the research phase, the outline, writing (draft after draft after draft, informed by reader feedback), cover/layout design brainstorming and iterations, formatting, launching, marketing, and who knows, maybe updates/future editions.

Thank yous

Jenn Paul Glaser, former student turned project partner, who designed this book inside and out. She and I spent a lot of time collaborating in Boulder coffee shops (a shout out to Ozo's and Flatiron Coffee!), and I loved every minute of it. Writing a book can be a weird, solitary experience, but once Jenn was on board I never felt alone. (And the book is freakin' beautiful!) I may have to write another one so I have an excuse to work with her again.

Everyone who read early drafts of this book and sent me comments, corrections, and personal stories: Karen Aller, Mike Benson, Russell Friesen, Lauren Gombas, Kathy LeMunyon, Jenni Lillie, Mandy Linton, Julie Mittel, and Courtney Raelynn. I was so touched that they all volunteered their time and expertise to help me out. The book is much better because of their feedback. (Your bottles of wine are on the way!)

My dad, Pete, who read the manuscript the same day I sent it out to my posse and was the very first person to send me feedback. I incorporated all of it except the part where he suggested that I cut back on the profanity. (Sorry, Dad, there's really no good substitute for the word "asshole.")

My entire family, for not getting mad when I ignored Christmas 2017 to focus on this book. I still owe some nephews gift cards.

Everyone who ever hired me for a UX job (and everyone who didn't) – it was all fodder for this book.

Bruce, Zach, and Donna from Boulder Digital Arts, for taking a chance on me as your UI/UX design instructor and for all the support you guys have provided (to me and the students).

Meredith Rafter, who consulted with me on how to be a better career coach for my BDA students and ultimately inspired me to write this book.

Tara Gentile, who also inspired this book without even knowing it through her CreativeLive class, "How to Write and Publish an eBook." Her assignment – write a 10,000-word ebook about something you already know. I got caught up in the subject and wrote an extra 20,000 words.

And finally, my students, for asking all those hard questions.

Resources

Books to Teach and Inspire You

Don't Make Me Think by Steve Krug

The Design of Everyday Things by Don Norman

The User Experience Team of One: A Research and Design Survival Guide by Leah Buley

Rocket Surgery Made Easy: The Do-It-Yourself Guide to Finding and Fixing Usability Problems by Steve Krug

A Project Guide to UX Design: For user experience designers in the field or in the making (2nd edition) by Russ Unger

UX for Beginners: A Crash Course in 100 Short Lessons by Joel Marsh

Discussing Design: Improving Communication and Collaboration through Critique by Adam Connor

Articulating Design Decisions: Communicate with Stakeholders, Keep Your Sanity, and Deliver the Best User Experience by Tom Greever

UX Strategy: How to Devise Innovative Digital Products that People Want by Jaime Levy

Badass: Making Users Awesome by Kathy Sierra

Experience Required: How to become a UX leader regardless of your role by Robert Hoekman Jr

100 Things Every Designer Needs to Know About People by Susan Weinschenk

Mapping Experiences: A Complete Guide to Creating Value through Journeys, Blueprints, and Diagrams by James Kalbach

The User's Journey: Storymapping Products That People Love by Donna Lichaw and Eva-Lotta Lamm

Web Form Design: Filling in the Blanks by Luke Wroblewski

Designing Web Interfaces: Principles and Patterns for Rich Interactions by Bill Scott and Theresa Neil

About Face: The Essentials of Interaction Design by Alan Cooper, Robert Reimann, David Cronin, and Christopher Noessel

The Elements of User Experience: User-Centered Design for the Web and Beyond (2nd Edition) by Jesse James Garrett

Evil by Design: Interaction Design to Lead Us into Temptation by Chris Nodder

Mobile Design Pattern Gallery by Theresa Neil

Tapworthy: Designing Great iPhone Apps by Josh Clark

Designing Your Life: How to Build a Well-Lived, Joyful Life by Bill Burnett and Dave Evans

Steal Like an Artist: 10 Things Nobody Told You About Being Creative by Austin Kleon

Show Your Work!: 10 Ways to Share Your Creativity and Get Discovered by Austin Kleon

Lean UX: Applying Lean Principles to Improve User Experience by Jeff Gothelf and Josh Seiden

The Lean Startup: How Today's Entrepreneurs Use Continuous Innovation to Create Radically Successful Businesses by Eric Ries

Letting Go of the Words, Second Edition: Writing Web Content that Works by Janice (Ginny) Redish

Articles Referenced

Amy Elisa Jackson, "15 More Companies That No Longer Require a Degree—Apply Now," Glassdoor.com, Jan 5, 2018, *https://www.glassdoor.com/blog/no-degree-required/?utm_source=newsletter&utm_medium=email&utm_content=15_jobs_no_degree&utm_campaign=jan18_us.*

Alison Green, "How to list accomplishments on your resume when your job doesn't have easy measures," Ask a Manager blog, June 24, 2013, *http://www.askamanager.org/2013/06/how-to-list-accomplishments-on-your-resume-when-your-job-doesnt-have-easy-measures.html.*

Simon Pan, "Great Design Portfolios Are Great Stories," Medium.com, Feb 24, 2015, *https://medium.com/interactive-mind/great-design-portfolios-are-great-stories-7bb2617cd7ab.*

Modicum, "The Rise of the UX Gold Rush," *Forbes*, July 15, 2017, *https://www.forbes.com/sites/propointgraphics/2017/07/15/the-rise-of-the-ux-goldrush/#2bf2d2958292.*

Kathryn Minshew, "A Simple Formula for Answering "Tell Me About Yourself," TheMuse.com, *https://www.themuse.com/advice/a-simple-formula-for-answering-tell-me-about-yourself.*

Justin Baker, "2018's UX Designer Salary Forecast," Medium.com, Nov 26, 2017, *https://medium.muz.li/2018s-ux-designer-salary-forecast-32ccc1dfcd5f.*

Adam Bryant, "In Head-Hunting, Big Data May Not Be Such a Big Deal," *New York Times*, June 19, 2013, *http://www.nytimes.com/2013/06/20/business/in-head-hunting-big-data-may-not-be-such-a-big-deal.html?pagewanted=all.*

Weston Karnes, "Learnings from Product Design Interviews," Medium.com, Oct 3, 2017, *https://medium.com/@westonkarnes/ learnings-from-product-design-interviews-7a494d531960*.

Jakob Nielsen, "Corporate UX Maturity: Stages 1-4," nngroup.com, Apr 24, 2006, *https://www.nngroup.com/articles/ux-maturity-stages-1-4/*.

Jakob Nielsen, "Corporate UX Maturity: Stages 5-8," nngroup.com, May 1, 2006, *https://www.nngroup.com/articles/ux-maturity-stages-5-8/*.

Jakob Nielsen, "Salary Trends for UX Professionals," nngroup. com, Jan 2, 2015, *https://www.nngroup.com/articles/ salary-trends-usability-professionals/*.

UXPin, "Enterprise UX Industry Report 2017-2018," UXPin.com, *https:// www.uxpin.com/enterprise-ux-design-2017-2018-industry-report*.

Portfolio sites
Simon Pan, Uber case study, *http://simonpan.com/work/uber/*.

Websites
Ask a Manager, *http://askamanager.com*
Glassdoor, *http://glassdoor.com*
Indeed, *http://indeed.com*
LinkedIn, *http://linkedin.com*
Meetup, *http://meetup.com*
Medium, *http://medium.com*
Monster, *http://monster.com*
Nielsen Norman Group, *http://nngroup.com*
UserTesting, *http://usertesting.com*
UX Mastery, *http://uxmastery.com*

Classes
Boulder Digital Arts, *http://www.boulderdigitalarts.com/training/details. php?offering=395*

Center Centre, *http://centercentre.com/program.*

General Assembly, *http://generalassemb.ly/education/user-experience-design.*

Lynda.com , *http://lynda.com/User-Experience-training-tutorials/97-0. html*

Springboard, *http://www.springboard.com/workshops/ux-design.*

User Experience Program, *http://www.springboard.com/learning-paths/user-experience-design/.*

Udemy, *http://udemy.com.* Anything by David Travis is good, start with his course *"User Experience (UX): The Ultimate Guide to Usability and UX,"* *http://www.udemy.com/ultimate-guide-to-ux/.*

UIE's All You Can Learn, *http://aycl.uie.com*

Tools

Adobe Creative Cloud, *http://adobe.com/creativecloud/desktop-app.htm*l.

Appear.in, video collaboration, *http://appear.in/.*

Axure, *http://axure.com.*

Balsamiq, *http://balsamiq.com.*

Bluehost web hosting, *http://bluehost.com*

Envato Market's themeforest (great WordPress themes), *http://themeforest. net/category/wordpress.*

Google Analytics, *http://www.google.com/analytics/.*

Google fonts, *http://fonts.google.com/*

Google Hangouts, *http://hangouts.google.com/.*

InVision, *http://invisionapp.com.*

Pixabay, free stock photos and images, *http://pixabay.com.*

Sketch, *http://sketchapp.com.*

Skype, *http://skype.com.*

Slack, *http://slack.com.*

UXPin, *http://uxpin.com.*

HOW TO GET A UX DESIGN JOB

Made in the USA
Monee, IL
13 January 2021

57299027R00079